T5-DHI-502

A WORD IN EDGEWISE

MARTHA WEGNER

Life in between
Raising Kids,
Keeping a Home,
and Staying Sane

Word in Edgewise © 2016 Martha Wegner

These essays have appeared over the years in over 100 publications, including *Big Apple Parent, San Diego Family,* and the *Minneapolis Star Tribune.*

All rights reserved. No part of this book may be reproduced by any mechanical, photographic, or electronic process, or in the form of a phonographic recording, nor may it be stored in a retrieval system, transmitted, or otherwise be copied for public or private use, other than for "fair use" as brief quotations embodied in articles and reviews without prior written permission of the publisher.

ISBN 13: 978-1-59298-747-4

Library of Congress Catalog Number: 2016908608

Printed in the United States of America

First Printing: 2016

20 19 18 17 16   5 4 3 2 1

Cover and interior design by Laura Drew.

Beaver's Pond Press
7108 Ohms Lane
Edina, MN 55439–2129
952-829-8818
www.beaverspondpress.com

For John

If home is where the heart is, then you are my home.

TABLE OF CONTENTS

PREFACE

I count my years as a young wife and mother as the most satisfying and joyful of my life. At the same time, raising children and keeping a household together were some of the most challenging experiences of my life. I worked on keeping my sanity (and my sense of humor) in the same way I dealt with all occurrences: I wrote. And then I sent these essays off to various magazines and newspapers. To my delight, they were published; it turns out these experiences were not all that unique. It seems we're all just trying to find a way to stay sane in the midst of raising children and keeping a house.

If you're in the middle of it, take heart: you will get through it.

If you're, like me, finally finished, congratulations. We did it.

GOTTA START A NEW LIFE

There we were, having another lazy Sunday afternoon at home. How does your family spend Sunday afternoon? I suppose you'll say reading the paper, going on a pleasant family outing, watching football with friends, playing board games with the kids. Not this family. On that particular day we were working and cleaning and arguing. I was carrying yet another load of laundry downstairs, our daughter was complaining loudly about how much she hated piano, and our son was crying because there's nothing good on TV Sunday afternoons. Above this din of domesticity my husband was actually trying to vacuum the family room floor. Finally, in exasperation, he put down the vacuum and said, "Do you remember that song from our teenage years, the one where the guy says, 'Tell my family I won't be coming home; gotta start a new life.' Do you ever feel the same way?"

To which I heartily responded, "Yes!" as I dropped the laundry bucket and broke out into full song. The kids interrupted their strain of complaint long enough to hear a few lines, and then the chain of whining started all over again.

My husband then asked, "You know, I don't know why that guy got to leave. You don't just pick up and go, do you?"

I knew why the guy left. He found his wife "in the arms of another man." My husband mused, "Hmmm, so that guy had an excuse to leave…" He didn't have to finish his sentence. We, on the other hand, do not have an excuse to leave. We bore these children; we raise these children. And we stick with them. Through the complaints, the tears, the just plain bad moods. And hopefully through the successes, the smiles, and the affection they sometimes bestow on us. Only right then, that good stuff was pretty hard to remember.

So my husband once again picked up the vacuum. I put down the microphone and picked up the laundry basket, and the kids resumed their complaints. But not before Dad and Mom took a little dance step together, holding each other's hands and smiling while Mom sang that old familiar song. Because, even if we can't start a new life, we can still laugh about the one we're in.

THE CHANGES THEY BRING

I was sitting at a wine bar with a friend of mine the other night. She had just announced to me that she was pregnant, and of course she was just so happy, as she deserved to be. Then she leaned into me, placing her newly manicured fingers on the arm of my blouse, the one with the macaroni and cheese stain, and asked, "Does your life change a lot when you have a baby?" I sat speechless as visions of bottles, diapers, delirious moments brought on by lack of sleep, and *all that crying* flooded my brain.

I smiled weakly, "Well, things will be a little different for you." This, spoken to half of a high-powered couple with lots of money, good jobs, and plenty of time for leisure activities. This woman had just finished telling me how she and her husband usually get home from work around 6:30, open a bottle of wine, and cook a meal together. Then they might go for a walk around the lake, perhaps a massage, maybe take in a movie.

Where do I begin to tell her how different her life will be? How she can kiss those romantic leisurely meals good-bye for the next eighteen years? How any action that used to be done on impulse will now require a call to at least three different babysitters? This couple had just returned from a week's vacation on a private boat off the Great Barrier Reef, for Pete's sake! Yes, I do believe life will change for them.

Now I need to tell a little truth here. I hope their life really, really changes. Because I am so envious of them, I can't see straight. They get to go to California to run in a marathon, while I spend my weekend running after kids. They get to see the latest R-rated action movie while I'm stuck with G-rated animated fare. They take a vacation to Australia; I go to the Wisconsin Dells. Darn, I'm jealous. So I must admit that in my green-eyed envy, I want them to live the life of drudgery we parents all live.

But in my good moments I also have nobler reasons for hoping their lives will change. How do I begin to describe the joy this child will bring? Along with all the compromises and concessions, there is indescribable joy.

As I took my last sip of wine, my friend finished off her club soda. I was off to relieve the babysitter. My friend was probably off to do a little shopping before heading home for some late night TV. As I entered my sleeping children's rooms I thought, of course, "My life has changed. I do make accommodations for the sake of my children in many aspects of my life." But as I looked at their sweet faces, I knew, as any parent does, it's all worth it.

DROWNING IN A SEA OF TALKERS

"Mom, are you listening to me?" I turn around once again to face my youngest child.

"Of course I'm listening to you. Aren't I always listening to you?" Undaunted by the less-than-positive tone in my voice, my son proceeds to tell me his story about… let's see, is it Pokémon, a monster, perhaps that bully at preschool? Maybe it's about a dream he had, what he wants to be when he grows up, perhaps this really long story about what he did when he was a little boy. If he pauses long enough to take a breath, his sister barges in with one of her tales. Perhaps it's softball, her anxiety over school, the entire plot of the latest book she just finished. Now wait, there's a little silence— soon to be filled by their father. The latest problem at work, some political comment about the news. Maybe he wishes to tell me his travel schedule for the next four and a half years. No matter, I just nod my head and say "Uh-huh." They don't need much more. I do have to assign them places in the listening line: "OK, now I need to listen to what David has been trying to say to me. Oh—hold on, David, Christine is complaining

6

because I cut her off. Sorry, John, I don't have my weekly planner, can you just hold on to that story?" You get the not-so-pretty picture. I swear I'm going to get one of those swivel armchairs installed in the passenger seat of our next car; anything to save my neck from a permanent crick caused by constantly turning to hear the next discourse.

I took a personality test called the Myers-Briggs Type Indicator a couple of years ago at my job. Not too surprisingly, on the introvert-extrovert section of the test, I was nearly off the scale for introversion. That means I get my energy from silence. Nothing brings tears of joy to my eyes faster than the thought of being alone in the house with a bubble bath and a good book.

Soon after, my husband took the same test. Again, not surprisingly, I learned that I had hitched myself to an extrovert. Extroverts get their energy from others! My extrovert wouldn't know what to do with himself if he were left in a quiet house. I'm sure he'd call his mother, the original extrovert. Or he'd track me down, just so he could talk.

My mother tells me that when I was a child, she could just put me on the floor and I would play by myself. I have visions of her running around after my two very active older sisters while I contently strung beads and listened to music. I imagine she had to remember to put me to bed!

So when I had children I expected the same. What I found out after my daughter's birth was that I had unknowingly produced another extrovert. She needed to tell me everything, show me everything ("Yes, that is so wonderful," I'd say, even if I had seen that dance step 200 times!). Still, I harbored hopes for her brother, who came along four years later. David and I were going to be the quiet ones.

No such luck. From the time he was born, he has had to have an audience for everything he experiences. And that audience is me. I am not kidding when I say I have seen "how high he can jump" nearly every day since he turned three. I have heard every dream. Seen every letter he has written. When out of sheer exhaustion I say to my children, "Go play by yourselves!," they give me a look of such utter amazement. I might as well be telling them to go speak Russian to the neighbors.

Here's the real rub. I think extroverts are out to get us introverts. I have evidence of it in my own family. You see, they don't get their energy from each other. They get it from me! Every day, they drain me dry. My children never demand that their dad watch or comment or laugh. No, it's got to be mama. She is the best audience. And their dad is a coconspirator. He'll wait, if he has to. He'll wait till the kids are in bed and I have finally picked up that blessed book for my fifteen minutes of silence. Then he'll attack. "You won't believe what happened at work today."

I sigh and put down my book. I nod and say, "Oh," and smile, laugh, or scowl at the appropriate places. Then it's time for bed—I've gotta rest up if I'm going to be a good audience tomorrow.

MY HEALTHY CHILD

My son has been given a clean bill of health from his surgeon. He's fine. No athletic restrictions, no more surgeries, no more ultrasounds, and no more doctor visits for two years. I sit up attentively, leaning forward. "Are you sure?"

The doctor nods, giving me a gift, wrapped up in a smile. "I'm sure." I don't dare lean back and sigh until he has signed the chart, put it back in its place, and left the room. David continues his motor-driven dinosaur sounds on the floor while I sit with tears welling up in my eyes. He's healthy... He's healthy... The words are sweet and bear repeating.

Two years ago, at the age of two and a half, David started getting sick. Weekly, he had unexplained vomiting that would last all night. By midmorning he was up and about, as if nothing had happened, leaving his bleary-eyed parents scratching their heads and wondering, "Could this be yet another virus?" After six months of this, including visits to the doctor and emergency rooms (during one such visit he was declared to be constipated), and lots of dirty bed sheets, I declared I'd had enough. There was something wrong with this kid, and I wasn't leaving my pediatrician's office until I knew what it was. And find out we did. It was his kidney, a serious problem, but an operable one. Lucky for us, surgery fixed it. The doctor was able to repair the damaged kidney. Now we just go in every six months for an ultrasound and a doctor visit. And with every visit I hold my breath. I'm sure the doctor will say something else is wrong with my sweet boy's perfect body, and I am prepared to weep. But he doesn't. It's always fine. His body has been made perfect again.

There are three things I've learned from this experience. First, doctors deserve to be paid as much as they are. That this man could cut open my child's body and repair a tiny vital organ, essentially saving his life, is beyond my imagination. I hope he is a millionaire.

Second, children's bodies are miracles. When my son runs around in circles after his sister, then stops long enough for me to wipe his nose or give him a drink of water, I often put my hand over his chest to hold him still. Under my fingers I feel a heartbeat, a tiny rapid rhythm. A miracle. And I pray to God that that little vulnerable heartbeat never stops, just as I pray the rest of his body keeps going. If we are unsure about the miracle of our children's bodies, we just need to spend an afternoon in a children's ward of a hospital. There we will see bald-headed kids wheeling IV stands down the hall, their weary parents trailing behind. These parents will tell us about the miracle of a healthy body.

Finally, we need to treat our children well. This is for the lady at the ice rink yesterday who was screaming into her child's ear, until he cried; I want her and all of us to know that our children are fragile beings that could fall ill at any minute. They need our discipline and our lessons, but they don't need our anger. We'll never know if what we say to them might be the last words they hear.

The doctor has left, we are free to go home. So I gather my child, my feelings of relief, and the lessons I have learned. My son gathers his sucker. We put away the dinosaurs and the truck, and make our way down the hall. He asks, "Do I have to have any more surgery?"

I say, "No. We're done." I smile. He smiles. He holds my hand as we cross the street to the parking lot. And I feel so blessed.

LOST AND FOUND

Today's fiasco: not being able to find those five-pound weights. That's right, mama has finally gotten down to the basement to *work out* and someone has stolen her weights. Here I am, sitting on my bench, ready to begin my biweekly, or perhaps monthly workout. My biceps are rippling in anticipation. And the weights are gone.

The accusations fly. Well, actually they just start as suggestions. First I go after my husband, who has this really annoying habit of picking things up and trying to organize our limited space. I always say, why pick it up, when you're sure to use it again in the next week? But I figure he's found a "space" for these little errant objects. Perhaps in a cupboard, dear? A closet? No way, he assures me, he would never meddle with my weights.

OK, with perhaps a slightly sharper tone, I go after my daughter. She is eight years old, and I'm just convinced she must have moved them during her last workout (I'm kidding, by the way). She insists she never saw them either. OK, the world is on hold while we find the weights. By now, these little Target cheapies have taken on a value beyond gold. Armies of search teams are sent out. My daughter digs through the dress-up box, slippers and hats flying. My husband is banished to the dreaded furnace room, where nobody outside of the Orkin man would venture. I myself pace back and forth around the room, occasionally flinging open a cupboard here and there, all the while muttering (not too softly), "Wouldn't it be nice if SOMETHING of mine in this house weren't taken, eaten, or stepped on?"

We don't find them that day. My husband comforts me, "They'll show up soon, honey, I just know they will." His voice comes straight out of a *Lassie* rerun, and it makes me feel like he's secretly hidden the weights and won't fess up. The look on my face tells him it's probably best to just let them be found.

And found they are. The next day my husband gets it in his head to look in one more place: the ice cream truck. You see, we have this little, plastic, toy ice cream truck that the kids are both really too old to be tooling around in. But the irresistible thing about this vehicle is that its seat lifts up, offering a cool little place to stash things, like keys, stuffed animals, and five-pound weights. Sure enough, inside the trunk are the missing weights. My four-year-old son's been busted.

The three of us storm into the family room to interrogate him. "Did you or did you not take those weights?"

He looks away from the TV long enough to say, "Sure I did. I was going to sell them later." And he resumes his viewing. We three are left open-mouthed and dumbstruck. Why didn't we think to ask him in the first place? How is it that the three of us spent our Saturday morning accusing each other of theft, forgetfulness, and even a little manipulation while the criminal sat and watched cartoons and ate Cheerios?

When I look back on that Saturday, I wonder, who got the better part of that day? The crabby trio, searching furtively for those weights, or the kid who sat back and waited for the dust to settle? Of course he knew where they were. But no one thought to ask him.

BLINDED BY THE MESS

There it sits. The bottle of children's cough syrup. Sticky rivulets of red goo have flowed down its side, creating a perfectly round red ring on my white kitchen counter. In fact, this bottle has been sitting there for approximately three weeks, ever since my husband administered the offending liquid to our sick child. He did not put the medicine back into the medicine cabinet, and so it will stay... on the kitchen counter. Every day I watch it, to see if it'll ever get put away. My money says it will still be sitting there this summer. This bottle is an integral part of a two-way domestic dispute. The other player: my partner of twenty-five years, also known as my husband, John.

I will not put the bottle away. Just as I will not put away my son's drawing pad, and I will not put away my daughter's sweatshirt. The members of my family are a responsible lot—at least they're supposed to be, and if I keep cleaning up their clutter, how will they ever learn to do it alone? There is only one problem to this method of teaching: it does not work. Because soon that drawing pad just becomes part of the scenery. We eat meals around this pad. The sweatshirt stays draped over the kitchen chair; I think my daughter uses it for cushioning. And I swear that, soon, the neglected bottle on the counter will be engulfed by vines from the ivy plant sitting next to it. Just another decorative item in the kitchen.

In the case of the cough medicine, I decided to cheat a little and give my husband a nudge: "You know, the cough syrup belongs in the medicine cabinet. It's probably time to put it away, since David is no longer coughing." (OK, so the hint was *way* obvious, but some people just need to be hit over the head.) He replied in this affected innocent tone, "Oh, I thought you were going to use it, so I left it out." What? Like I might just come down with a hacking cough this very evening?

John did not take the hint. He has now become blind to the bottle, just as we have all become blind to the swimming goggles sitting in the corner since last summer, the camera (from our trip this fall), and the *People* magazine from last summer.

Perhaps it's a survival mechanism. Maybe we'd be just a little crazy if every day we had to face these messes. More likely, we are just lazy, and don't feel like throwing that magazine away. So our psyches develop an elaborate system to help us in our denial of the clutter surrounding us.

My husband tells me that I am every bit as guilty of this clutter blindness as he is. I have no idea what he is talking about. I don't see a mess.

In any case, we are surrounded by our stuff, a tradition we have maintained for the last twenty-five years. And I don't see it ending soon.

WE HAVE A NEW CHILD
AT OUR HOUSE

We have a new child at our house. He is a four-and-a-half, almost five-year-old boy. He is happy; he is agreeable. He says "OK" to almost all of my requests. If he loses his temper, he apologizes afterward. He hugs my neck and calls me "Mommy Love-Love." He embraces his big sister and asks her what she wants to play.

And he draws. He draws Christmas trees with all the bulbs and wires connected. Fireplaces with orange and red flames and brown logs, chimneys with gray smoke leading up to the sun. He draws bunnies with pink-lined ears under the trees, sheep on the planet Mars out in space, and red pebbles on the ground. He draws his father with a tornado coming out of his tummy. He draws little mice hiding in the corner. He draws flowers, and sharks and flags and refrigerators full of food, and buildings with writing on the sides and ladders to the roof. His drawings cover the family room walls and have now emigrated to his bedroom walls.

This new child came from his old self. The one who said "No" to everything, who ate only candy, who threw a tantrum at the idea of changing out of his pajamas. The child who had no trouble expressing hatred for whomever in his family had the audacity to suggest he wash his hands or turn off the TV. This old self crumbled into tears when he "forgot what he was going to say," yelled with rage when a vegetable touched his peanut butter sandwich. And this old child never drew a picture. He said he didn't know how to draw, and he wasn't going to try.

Then one day, about a month ago, my new child walked in the door. He looked the same, except for the absence of a scowl. He had in his hand a picture of a Christmas tree he had stenciled at preschool. He said he wanted to "add a few things." He added. Ornaments, presents, bulbs, chimneys, sky. Since then he has had to create daily. The markers are never put away. His father, sister, and I are astounded. And we are silent. No use jinxing our good fortune.

In the "bad child days," I desperately e-mailed a friend of mine who happens to be a "parent-infant specialist" (what I wouldn't give for that moniker), to ask her for advice. She told me that David had been in a state of disequilibrium. And I gotta say that was one accurate term. His world was one big state of disequilibrium, and nothing I could do or say for him would make it right. Now she tells me he is in a stage of "expansion." And I say, "Great!" Then I say, "How long will it last?" And, "Can I bottle it?" Because I'm telling you, this is pure joy. It makes it OK to be a parent again.

It is as if my son has given birth to this new self. Like giving birth, it was a painful, desperate, terrifying time for all of us. Then one day the new baby walks in the door. He has emerged. His sweet pink face smiling, and we can almost forget the unbearable pain it took to get there.

This might all have a happy ending if I wasn't sure, based on the books and my own experience, that this new child just might go the way of the horrendous child he replaced. You see, the experts tell us these stages are temporary, fleeting, always cycling. Darn it. Like a tantruming child myself I pound my fist and say, "I want him to stay this way!" But no, he will surely cycle out. A new child, perhaps a little more difficult, perhaps a lot more difficult will take his place. But, keep reading, those same experts tell us that just as he cycles into a more difficult stage, so will he cycle back into this sweet creative energy we call David.

In the meantime, I am rushing to get more markers and paper. He just thought of a new idea: it's a picture of Earth, and Mars, and underneath is a lion and he's going to eat the bad guy, and... and...

I do so love this stage. I'll take it while I can. And I'll try to remember it when the "bad child days" return.

THE REFEREE

My friend Nancy tells me that when her kids get home from school each day she dons her striped referee jersey and gets out the whistle. Let the arguments begin! I know just what she means. And you know what the experts tell us? Don't get involved. Let them settle their own arguments. I do try. I try until I am sure blood is going to flow from one of their young bodies; I try until the volume and pitch just shock my brain into action. Then I do what every other parent does: I get smack dab in the middle of it. Whistle blowing, arms waving, mouth screaming.

Last week my children discovered a most coveted possession: a stick. Mind you, a *twelve-inch* stick. Immediately an argument began as to just whose stick this was. You see, my daughter saw it while playing on the swing set, but my son ran over it, and his foot touched it. She was the first one to pick it up, but, she let it go, and he picked it up. You're probably getting the idea, and it's all too familiar. There are rules in Kid Land that I am still trying to figure out, or remember from my own childhood. But they include the following: if you want the object, even slightly, it is worth fighting for. No amount of reasoning will change that. Also, if you ever touched, saw, or even expressed a desire for an object, it is yours.

So, you see how the stick fits into all this. They both wanted it, they both claimed it, and they were going to fight to the bitter end for it!

Just then my sister called from out of town. Over pleasant chat I could be heard to scream, hand over the receiver, at punctuated intervals: "Give the stick to your brother! Do it now!"; an occasional plea: "David, now Christine is crying, can she just play with it?"; then into a threat: "Stop fighting over that stick or I'll take it away from both of you!"

My sister calmly observed, "This reminds me of the story of King Solomon. You should look that up in the Bible."

You know, many of us consult Dr. Spock or any one of the many childhood gurus, but I thought, "Why not? I'll just go right to the top and consult the Big Guy." And there it was, right in the Books of Kings.

It turns out, arguments like this have been happening since the dawn of time. Kind of a comfort to me, I must admit. Essentially, Solomon had to act as referee to two women over who possessed a baby. King Solomon said, "Divide the baby in half," at which point the real mother said, "Oh no, sir! Give her the child—don't kill him!" Thus we have the Wisdom of Solomon.

I told a group of parents at a church luncheon about the big stick argument, and about how King Solomon might have solved it. One woman in the group was from Ecuador. She said, in her clipped rapid English, "You know, I agree with King Solomon. When my sister and I used to argue over a doll, my mom used to rip the doll in half. And that was the end of that." She demonstrated with a quick imaginary split of the hands. Each one of us stopped mid-chew to contemplate such a scene: two very shocked little girls looking at half a doll, stuffing falling onto the floor, limp limbs hanging. Did they cry, did they scream? We'll never know, but one thing is for sure: they never fought over an object again.

So, next time, will I crack that now long-forgotten stick over my knee? Walk away from the stunned silence and inevitable tears, knowing "that was the end of that"? Or will I continue to holler, beg, and threaten during these incessant kid battles?

I could always do what the experts say: stay out of it. I guess that's why they're the experts, and I'm not.

The thought of a broken stick, a torn doll, a smashed bicycle is more than I can bear. Actually, the look on my kids' faces is more than I can bear. So for now, I keep that whistle in my back pocket, the off-sides flag tucked into my waistband. And I really, really will try to stay out of it. And I'll hope and pray that someday soon God will grant me the Wisdom of Solomon.

MY LIFE WITH A DOG

My family has embarked on a mission. It's called, "Do anything you can to persuade Mom to get a dog, because we can't be happy children without one." Like a verbal form of Chinese water torture, they work me. "Oh"— followed by a long, mournful sigh—"I wish we had a dog. Then I would have someone to _____." Fill in the blank with "love," "play with," "be friends with," "cuddle with," "sleep with," "run away with"— you get the idea.

Because I am under the spell of two sighing children (and a husband who refuses to get involved in this latest attack on his wife), I felt it was time to take my questions public. I polled the dog owners in my life. The question was simple: what are the good and the bad things about having a dog? I am now happy to give you the results of this informal and unbiased survey. Because I am trying to illuminate the reasons why I am *not* getting a dog, I will start with the negatives: Dog hair. Everywhere. Picking up dog poop. Add to this, dirty paws on the white carpet, chewed furniture, and having to figure out what to do with Fido when going out of town. Oh, and did I mention the expense, the running away, and the obedience classes? The list goes on. For good measure my sister adds: "Puking right as we're sitting down to Thanksgiving supper at Mom's house." This is true. I was there.

My friend Marianne adds one more illuminating detail: don't think for one minute, no matter how old your children are, no matter how responsible they are, that they will take care of the dog. They won't. This dog will be yours.

OK, let's move on to the positive aspects, shall we? According to my sources, even if the kids think the dog is theirs, you and the pooch will know the truth. Because you will be its primary caregiver, you, as my friend tells it, will become the alpha female. You, dear reader, will be the big kahuna, the main rule maker, the all-wise authority, and *won't that feel great*? OK, so now the dog is looking a little more appealing. A sweet little pooch who looks up into my eyes and accepts and knows (without argument, I might add) that I am queen of the household might not be that bad after all.

Still, I find myself searching for reasons not to give in to these incessant pleas. And then it occurs to me: looking for reasons not to get a dog is almost like looking for reasons not to have a kid. I could list all the negatives of child-rearing, starting with sleepless nights and ending with curfew fights. But I can't really list all the immeasurable things having children has added to my life. Maybe dog ownership is intangible like that.

Because although my friends and siblings can tell me all the reasons why I shouldn't own a dog, they do so while cuddling their dogs. The truth is that, like children, pooches love you no matter what and add happiness to your life.

You can tell my resolve is cracking. Just don't tell my kids.

MY JOURNEY TO HOME
IMPROVEMENT
*(Or How an Otherwise Intelligent
Woman Lost Her Way)*

Spring has finally arrived, and with it comes warm weather and the chance to rebuild and repair that which winter has destroyed. If you're like me, you can hardly wait to get some bids and get started on that new remodeling job. But before you rush into your next home improvement project, please take the time to read my family's tale of woe. Learn from our mistakes. The names in this story have been changed to protect the not-so-innocent.

It started out so simply. We needed a windowsill replaced. One windowsill. Our usual fix-it guy was overbooked, so he sent his cousin Bobby in his place. Bobby did good work, even if my kids could have done without having to look at his nipple ring every day (couldn't he have worn a shirt?). Bobby then invited his buddy Frank to help him with the job. And although my children were disgusted by his knocked-out front teeth and less-than-pleasant odor, Frank did even better work than Bobby. In the end, we were very pleased with the results. Nice sill, nice cleanup. This leads us to our first lesson.

Lesson #1: Do only what you set out to do.

We should have left it at that. Fix the windowsill and be done. Oh, but Frank noticed we needed a new screen in the family room; the next day he saw that we needed a new dryer vent. Soon we needed to replace a cracked window and the house needed to be painted. And then the *pièce de résistance*: "Those kids of yours deserve a playhouse, and we know how to do it." I saw my kids with their noses pressed against the screen (they were a little bit afraid of these guys, so they stayed inside), nodding their heads emphatically. Who was I to deny these children their childhood dream? "Sure," I said, "let's do it all!" And that's where things fell apart. Leading us to…

Lesson #2: When someone leaves in the middle of a job, chances are very good that he is not coming back.

The painting was well underway, and Bobby and Frank had started work on the screen, vent, and window. They were assembling the materials for the playhouse. Then, one day they just stopped showing up. Every day I called. And every day they said they were coming.

They didn't. I begged. I pleaded. I used guilt, as in "My poor kids are really counting on that playhouse." I tried anger, indignation, even sarcasm, saying "Oh, you're gonna show up today, huh? I'll believe it when I see it," in my best snarl. Nothing worked. And with every lie, every missed date, my family became uglier and uglier. Instead of walking through the door with "How was your day?" my husband's new question became "Did Curly and Moe show up?" We called them "Mutt and Jeff," "Frick and Frack," and soon my children just called them "The Idiots." We had been reduced to angry, vengeful persons; I didn't even recognize us anymore. Which leads to our next lesson…

Lesson #3: Don't give workers money for work they have not completed, even if they are really, really, nice guys.

As so often happens with people who inhabit one's home, it seems that Bobby and Frank and I kind of became buddies. We chatted and joked. They talked to the kids; they played with the dog. So when Bobby put on his shirt and asked me for just a *little* money to cover the paint, or Frank asked for *just twenty dollars* for for the playhouse's shingles, I obliged. I just took it off what I owed them for the done job. Well, the job wasn't not done, and I was left with a half-painted house, and less money. Now I was really, really angry. Leading us to the next lesson…

Lesson #4: Get the guy's last name.

My mother was horrified when I told her my story. She said, "Contact the Better Business Bureau!" Great idea, Mom, if I only I knew these guys' names. And by now their cell phones had been disconnected. I will end with the obvious. The one all you normal, intelligent, human beings know…

Lesson #5: Do what your mom and dad always taught you to do. Get the names of two to three reputable contractors, get some estimates, get some references, and then choose wisely.

When I look back on this story, I can't believe I let it happen. I guess I got caught up in the frenzy of home improvement, and lost my way.

Of course there are many good, reputable contractors out there. Take my experience to heart, and do your homework.

I'll be there right along with you, trying to find someone with a first *and* a last name who can paint, install a screen, a window, a dryer vent, and build a playhouse for my poor deprived children, who, a year later, are still waiting for their ultimate dream.

TRUE CONFESSIONS OF A MEDDLESOME MOM

The official order form arrived last week. There, in my smiling little Girl Scout's hand, the dreaded cookie sheet. "Wanna buy Thin Mints or Do-Si-Dos this year, Mom?" One look and I knew what I'd be doing the next few nights: walking the streets, peddling these little confections with her. She was the seller, but I was the coach. "Just one more house, honey. I know we can make the night's quota!"

On the way home from one of these little business forays, my daughter asked, "What did you and Grandma Jean do to sell cookies?" I had to think… and I didn't remember. I didn't remember because my mom wasn't there. She was home putting a diaper on my baby sister, or driving my teenage sister to the latest dance. The fact is, she didn't have time to get involved, but neither did any of the other harried mothers on our block. We kids were on our own, we all knew it, and that's the way life was. Kids did the selling of the cookies, they did their own homework, and they made their own social plans. Hard to believe, isn't it?

The great cookie caper was soon followed by the annual Inventors' Fair at school. My husband spent

Sunday afternoon shuttling our daughter from store to store, in addition to helping her with stitching, hammering, and gluing. When she stands up to receive her award for best invention and says, "I couldn't have done it without the help of my mom and dad!," she will not be kidding.

Back in the Dark Ages, parents would hardly even have known there was an Inventors' Fair going on. They cared; they were just too busy doing laundry or taking the little ones to the dentist to take over a kid's project. Besides, it *was* the kid's project, wasn't it?

Imagine little Thomas Edison laboring away over his newest invention. Do you suppose for one minute that his mom ran to the store to buy him just a little more wire? Do you think Amelia Earhart's parents signed her up for private after-school flying lessons? And how about little Alfred Fuller, the original Fuller Brush Man? Can you imagine his mama tagging along beside him as he peddled his wares, lugging the sack of bristles behind her? I think not.

When I write of the things I do for my daughter, I know I am not alone. I know you are out there now, helping your Boy Scout sell popcorn or your senior write her college applications. You can deny it, but you know you are one of us, you meddlesome parent, you. We need help. I propose we sign a pact: we will let our children do their own selling, their own projects, their own homework, and their own social plans. We'll keep our mouths shut, and our hands tied. Girl Scout cookies were meant for girls, not interfering mothers.

I'll sign it if you will. Right after I help my kindergartner collect one hundred objects for his latest class project. He couldn't possibly do it on his own, could he?

FOR THE LOVE OF LAUNDRY

A few years ago, my sister married into money. It just so happens she loved the guy too. When this unexpected extra income came her way, she was able to make some lifestyle choices, that is, she was able to "hire out" those household chores she no longer wished to do. She promptly hired someone to do her laundry. Yes, someone came into her house, sorted the laundry, put it into the machine, and turned it on. I'm sure this woman stayed around to dry everything just right, and iron the shirts and sheets before she went home to do her own laundry.

I was a bit baffled by this. Why, out of all the tedious, dreadful, tiresome cleaning tasks in your house, would you give away the laundry? Why not hire someone to vacuum or dust or wash windows? In fact, I can say that doing the laundry is about the only job that I actually enjoy, and I would be very sad to give up my machine to someone else.

I have a group of friends that agrees with me. We are a kind of secret laundry-loving society. We love washing the clothes, although we seldom admit it to anyone else. In fact, we feel a little guilty. Because when it's time to divvy up the chores, as in "I'll do the laundry, you do the toilets," we know we've gotten off with a good deal. No one should get full credit for doing such a pleasurable little task.

So, what is it that inspires us laundry lovers? First, and foremost, there is a finished product. And what a product it is. It is of course free of dirt, it smells fresh, and the cloth feels slightly stiff yet pleasingly soft in our hands when it comes out of our dryers. And it looks pretty darn impressive when we are walking from room to room, ceremoniously depositing the folded piles into each family member's drawer. Compare that to vacuuming, for which there is no definitive end product. There is always this lingering doubt, "Did I get under the chair? Guess I'd better do it *again*." Not to mention those pesky shreds that refuse to be sucked up. We have to bend down, loosen them, and force-feed them to the machine. All of which leaves us feeling that there may be other little errant shreds that we're missing. And then the kids run in with their muddy soccer shoes. There is definitely no end when it comes to vacuuming.

Then there's the exertion factor. Other than a few trips up and down the basement stairs, and a few twists of the wrist, doing laundry requires very little aerobic activity. It will never qualify for the exercise guidelines we're supposed to be following, you know the ten minutes, three times a day thing. Even pulling weeds and scrubbing the tub gives you more exercise. We laundry lovers are just fine with that. We really see no benefit to breaking a sweat.

Finally, there is the escape aspect. Many of us have our machines plugged into the deepest dankest corner of the basement, the place where no child (or spouse) will dare venture. One of my friends takes a magazine down there while she is "working." The kids are too afraid to bother her, for fear that the basement monsters will surely attack.

There are other chores that my friends recommend. One friend loves to sweep her floors by the entryway. For her, the act of sweeping fits the criteria of beginning and end. Sand on the floor one minute, gone the next. Also, there is a soothing feeling to the sweeping motion, a feeling I don't quite share, but I think I understand. Another friend loves to iron. She turns off the TV and radio, and, much as she is embarrassed to say it, feels she can "iron out her problems." I don't share her reflective feelings while I am trying to press a crease in my trousers, but I must admit I love the warmth on my fingers as they pass over newly ironed fabric.

Still, nothing compares to our laundry. If a pile of money comes my way soon you can bet I'll hire out the vacuuming or the window washing. Meanwhile, I'll be all by myself, down in the basement, pouring in the detergent, turning the knobs, and folding the sweet-smelling shirts.

VALENTINE LOVE

February has arrived, and I'm sorry to say we are greeting it with a groan. Even if the calendar says otherwise, we all know that February is the longest month of the year. The cold, gray days stretch endlessly in front of us, with nary a hint of spring blossoms. Add to that the realization that the holidays really are over, and the world looks bleak indeed. No more costumes, no more hand-traced turkeys, no more marshmallow snowmen. Gone is the holiday party, the anticipation, the "what did you get?" Oh, life is looking pretty gloomy right now.

On the other hand, we do have one little holiday to look forward to, and that is of course Valentine's Day. In my not-so-humble opinion, we really saved the best holiday for last.

So, what's the appeal? It's love, of course, the kind of love only a kid can give. I'm not talking puppy love here, the kind where the shy boy finally professes his true affection for the girl across the room. I'm talking about the kind of love that says, "You belong here. I'm glad you're here. Even if we're not the best of friends, there are things about you that I notice and like."

In my classroom, there are four rules for Valentine's Day. First and foremost, if you bring a valentine for one person, you bring one for each person. Second, you are required to sign the valentine. Third, and this is more encouragement than a rule, try to write a little note on the back, along with your signature. And finally, after you open a valentine, say thank you to the person who gave it to you.

At the appointed hour, we clear off the candy heart bingo games and the Styrofoam cups stained with raspberry punch, and we tear into our Valentine mailboxes. The silence is sweet as those first tiny envelopes are torn. Small smiles emerge and words of "thank you" are heard. The foil comes off chocolate hearts while laughter erupts as children watch the class bully open three Barbie valentines in a row.

From all this comes a sense of belonging, if only for a day. The girl that no one wants to sit next to now has a bag of twenty-six valentines, each signed by a kid, saying in effect, "I like you." The shy kid, who is afraid to speak up in class, sees that twenty-six kids like him too. And, if he's lucky, at least one of those kids has written something more, like "I think you're smart." The child who still can't read gets to hear that someone really likes the way he can draw Spider-Man. And yes, this teacher gets to read that at least some of her students really like, even love her. Seems to make it all worthwhile.

Perhaps we adults could take a lesson from our children's classrooms. Suppose bosses everywhere should proclaim, "This is Valentine's Day! Show your coworkers you care!" I'd be willing to bet that February 14th would take on a new level of importance in the workplace. For at least one hour on this day we would all get a chance to say "I love you," or at least "I like you, and I'm glad you're here." Finally we would get to hear what we're all yearning to hear year round.

February is indeed the darkest and bleakest of months. But the promise of spring lies in the affection we can express for each other on this best of all holidays. You can have your ornaments, your stuffed turkeys, your gory costumes, and your witch's brew. Just leave me Valentine's Day. I'll pop a candy heart in my mouth and revel in the knowledge that someone loves me, or at least likes me, just as our children have taught us to do so well.

ALPHA-DOG

He is driving us nuts, this cute little mutt who steals shoes, chews pillows, and growls at the children when they dare to wake him from his nap. My son yells in his most stern voice, finger wagging, "Chester, NO!" Chester sighs, and continues to chew the Lego piece.

In desperation, I put in a call to Grete. She is the DOG TRAINER.

Grete (pronounced "GRAY-ta") is everything her strong German name suggests. She is large—not in a literal sense, but more of a fills-the-room-with-her-presence sense. She does not find me at all entertaining, even when I throw out my best jokes. She is here to do work. I call her "Frau Grete" under my breath. I would not say it out loud; she would not think it was funny.

As Grete enters the room, Chester does his usual greeting, which involves jumping wildly into the air and onto the legs of the guest. This is met with a thrust-out knee, which certainly shocks our boy into submission. He then moves on to his next stunt: stealing the shoe. Just as he puts his mouth onto Grete's sensible leather boot, he is met with a withering look and a sound, deep in Grete's throat, an authoritative, "Uh-uh." Chester slinks away.

Grete instructs me to sit down so that we can go over the list of problem behaviors. Her solution: I simply *must* start acting like the "alpha." This, translated, means "number one dog." I need to let Chester know by my voice, my actions, and my body language that I am in charge. As if to prove her point, Chester trots in and actually sits at Grete's feet. He looks up at her adoringly, as if to say, "OK, what would you like me to do next? Perhaps roll over?" I am amazed. How can he be sitting at her feet, hanging on her every word? "It is simple," she says. "I am the alpha, and he knows it."

The funny thing is that I am pretty much the alpha with the rest of the beings in my household (meaning my husband and children). I yell, I scold, I give disapproving glances, and honestly, it does whip them into shape. So how come it doesn't work with this creature? Could it be that he is on to me? Is my alpha power just an illusion, soon to be dispelled when the kids reach adolescence and realize this is all a ruse?

I sure hope my family doesn't catch on. In the meantime, I've got work to do. Chester just stole another shoe. I can feel my alpha power slipping.

KEEPERS AND TOSSERS

To my way of thinking, there are two kinds of people in this world: the keepers and the tossers. You know you're a keeper if you still have your son's *Power Rangers* action figures stored in a box, and he has just started college. There are many, many keepers in this society of ours.

I used to be a keeper, until my house finally groaned, "Enough." Yes, my old house could not give me one more inch of space. After seven years of cramming just one more thing onto the shelves, my house was bulging. I would need to learn to become a tosser.

This shouldn't have been too difficult really, as I was raised by a woman who is a pretty darn good tosser herself. Never one for sentimentality, my mother threw out those things that had no immediate need, and I do mean immediate. If that jewelry box you made out of a shoebox and dried macaroni was important to you, you learned to keep it in the far reaches of your closet, or it would soon be part of the heaving bags of garbage carried out each week. Not that she was cruel; it was just that she had seven family members cycling their stuff through the house each day. Things had to be thrown so everyone could find his or her bed at night.

In order to become a tosser myself I needed a little help: I hired an organizer. This is a concept that my mother's generation cannot fathom. "You hire someone to help you get rid of junk? Call me! I've been tossing for years, and I come very, very cheap!" But that is not the way my generation does it. We pay someone to tell us what to toss and what to keep.

My organizer was relentless—kind, but relentless. If I hadn't used the toys or the clothes or the appliances in the past two years, I wasn't going to use them. Time to toss.

Once I got over the initial pain of seeing my son's plastic dinosaurs hit the donation heap, it actually became fun. As I tossed the items into the pile, it was nice to be reminded that I would *never* have to carry a squirming baby around in a front pack again. Fun to know I would *never* have to buckle a crying toddler into a car seat again. Ever. What a relief to know that I would not have to make a huge Waldorf salad to fill that monstrous salad bowl we got as a wedding gift all those years ago.

I have become so good at discarding that I actually look forward to holidays and birthdays. It gives me a chance to chuck those old toys and make room for the new. Clean drawers, clean shelves: what a sense of accomplishment.

I'll admit I've been a little overzealous in my mission at times, and I've had my share of remorse. I wish I hadn't tossed those old gray running shorts—I was actually looking for them the other day. My son was nearly in tears when he realized I had tossed his *G.I. Joe* doll—the one that he had never ever played with in his life. But the regret is nothing compared to the triumph I feel when a drawer is only half full instead of overflowing.

Recently, I visited my mom. She and Dad are downsizing, moving into a smaller house. She walked me down to the basement. I could see it in her eyes: she was on a tossing mission, and actually thought she could pass this junk on to me. "Here's a really nice tablecloth. How about this Christmas village? Need any extra light bulbs?" She hadn't realized that I had crossed over to her side. I had joined the ranks of the tossers, and I wasn't taking anything.

My unsuspecting sister, the one with the big empty new townhouse came down the stairs. "Whatcha doing?" she asked. Mom and I smiled conspiratorially. Mom handed her the black-and-white cow salt and pepper shakers while I showed her the old drapes which would look just perfect in her bedroom. Kathy thought she had hit the jackpot, and Mom and I got our tossing fix.

I predict that in seven years' time my sister's house will start bulging and complaining, and she will have to learn how to toss. She has no idea the pleasure that awaits her.

WE HAVEN'T GOT A PRAYER

I went to a retreat at my church Saturday morning. I arrived late, but not too late, considering I packed the children's suits for their swimming lessons, put in a load of laundry, helped my son find his long lost Lego piece, and fed the dog before I left.

Today's retreat topic: "Centering Prayer." My minister tells me it is the path to serenity, something that seems to be in short supply around here. The process is simple. You sit in silence for twenty minutes. That's it. Now, this seems to conjure up a vague memory. Let's see, my daughter is almost nine years old, which is exactly how long it's been since I've experienced this thing called silence. I do have a fuzzy recollection, just as I recall running two miles without having to stop and catch my breath, going to a movie without calling three babysitters first, and enjoying a little intimacy with my husband on a Sunday afternoon without a small fist banging on the bedroom door.

So, here is how the retreat begins. We watch this video of a monk who lives in Snowmass, Colorado. From what I can tell of this guy, he spends his life praying, eating, sleeping, and making videos. And let's just talk about Snowmass, Colorado. As in, ski resort. I am not exaggerating when I say it is the nearest thing to heaven that I've seen so far. So there he sits: no wife, no kids, no job, and probably very little laundry. Shall I go on? OK. No car pools, no piano lessons, and no cooking. Oh, I really must stop. Small wonder I want to reach into the TV set and hold him by the throat: "Hey buddy, walk a mile in my shoes!" He'd be crawling on his knees, whimpering like the rest of us, wondering where in the heck God went to.

But instead I restrain myself, and I try it out. I sit in silence for twenty minutes, doing my darndest to ignore all obsessive motherly thoughts. And I must admit it is nice. Very nice. Although approximately nineteen and a half of those twenty minutes are spent on grocery lists and my daughter's research report, I do experience a glimmer of real peace.

So, I am going to keep doing it. Because with practice, I'm told it will get easier. Those thirty seconds will grow to forty, maybe even more. Just because I'm a parent doesn't mean I can't have a little silence, serenity, and spirituality, right? I deserve it, and I'm gonna get it. Even if I have to do a load of laundry and take the dog to the vet first.

MAMA'S GOT HER RED DRESS ON

I'm getting ready to go out again. Red dress, silver hoop earrings, black pumps. My children plead, "Mom, do you have to go? Can't you just stay home tonight?" Lest you think I'm a middle-aged harlot sneaking off to the bars, let me set you straight. I'm off to choir. Yes, folks, mama's gone and joined up with a choir, and it's making my kids crazy.

My children have a picture of me that falls somewhere between reserved and downright stodgy. The fact that I am willing to stand up and croon my little heart out in front of an audience (wearing a red dress, no less) has turned this picture on its face.

Now, my children's view of me was not formed in a vacuum. I have never been one to get in front of a crowd and perform. I leave the embarrassing acts of entertainment to someone less self-conscious than me. But for some reason when I heard about this group of women who gather weekly to practice and perform, I just couldn't resist. Call it midlife madness; my kids, who have had to endure my morning songs while they eat their Cheerios, might call it punishment.

The ladies in this choir are very good singers, and what's best for me is they allowed me to join without a tryout. I bet there will be a change in future policy. They've come to realize that this newcomer knows little about music beyond elementary school piano lessons, and that I have never performed in a choir before. I'm not sure, but I think I notice them wincing ever so slightly when we hit those high notes.

When I first told my nine-year-old daughter that I had joined a choir, she looked at me in amazement. Not amazement of the joyful variety, more of the "You've got to be kidding" type. When I explained to her that I was doing this because it made me happy, she replied, "Couldn't you have done a sport, like tennis or something?" Yes, I guess tennis would have been less embarrassing for their little sensibilities, but it really just doesn't feel as good as singing "There Is Nothin' Like a Dame" with a sailor hat perched on my head.

My kids still turn their heads in embarrassment when I put on my red dress. This lady with the red dress and pumps (usually reserved for weddings and funerals) just can't be their mother. But in the end, amidst the snickers, I hope there will be some pride; pride that mama is doing what brings her joy, even if it is a little outside the box they have painted around me. And even if it is a little off-key.

TO EVERYTHING THERE IS A SEASON

There are few people who dislike Minnesota winters as much as I do. I hate the cold, the snow, the ice, the darned inconvenience of putting on layer after layer of polypropylene just to walk the dog. The dog looks up at me as I'm pulling the ski mask over my face as if to say, "Don't do this for me, that icy sidewalk freezes my paws, and you know I hate those silly dog boots. Just let me out to do my duty, and we'll call it a day." I can't for the life of me figure out why those early settlers chose to, well, settle here. Why build a log cabin in negative-twenty degree temps when they could have walked a couple hundred miles south and settled under a palm tree?

So you would think that with the chilly temps coming our way, I'd be in a perpetual state of sadness. I am. But truth be told, there is a certain amount of relief that blows in with the bitter north wind. You see, during the summer, I am guilt ridden. I am not a good gardener. I am not a good lawn person. My intentions are good... every day I wake up and tell myself that I will be attacking that crab grass. I will, I really will, prune the rose bush. Yes, today I will move the hosta.

I don't. I won't. More pressing matters enter in, like reading the latest mystery novel or chatting on the phone with my sister. Hence, the guilt.

So imagine my pleasure as the first flakes of snow fly. In an exaggerated gesture of disappointment I say to my husband, "Darn, that snow came a lot sooner than I expected. I had really hoped to get those bulbs planted. Doggone, guess it will have to wait until next year." I actually say this with a straight face. I have had many years of practice.

Yes, winter gives me a reprieve from the constant call of the yard. Once the bitter chill sets in, there's not much to do except shovel a little walkway for the dog, and settle in for a long winter's nap... guilt free.

But then the house starts calling. All those chores I ignored all summer because I was so busy, ahem, pulling weeds in the garden: the basement walls cry to be painted; the hinges on the closet door beg to be oiled; the spots on the carpet hint that I need to rent a Rug Doctor machine. I do some of it. But then I feel the need to catch up on the books I missed over the summer. And soon my sister calls.

Before I know it, the sun is not just shining; it is actually giving off heat. Spring is here, summer has arrived! I've missed my chances to paint and repair, darn it. But I just have to get outside and start fertilizing.

So, here it is, the real reason I stay in Minnesota, despite my intense aversion to the cold. It's the change of seasons and all the excuses that change brings for a procrastinator like me. I've discovered that if I wait around long enough, the season will change. And I may not have gotten a darn thing done in my house or yard, but there's always next year, right?

All of this comes with a price. I do have constant nagging guilt. I *should* be shoveling right now. I *should* be dividing my perennials. But as soon as my guilt gets the best of me and I pull all the right tools together, well, the season changes. I can put my shovel away for next year.

People tell me they love Minnesota for the change of seasons. I think they mean the beautiful new green of spring, the warmth of summer, the leaves in the fall, and the snow in the winter. I love Minnesota for the seasons too. I just think my reasons may differ a little.

Today the cold winds are blowing, and I can feel winter coming. Thank goodness. I still haven't quite gotten around to planting those bulbs.

THE STUFF OF MEMORIES

I called my sister last week, and asked her if she'd like to come visit us for the weekend. My husband and daughter were out of town, leaving me alone with my five-year-old son, David. Truth be told, I've been a little down in the dumps, and I thought a visit might just lift my tired spirits. Turns out my sister was feeling a little low herself. Her job had just been downsized, and once again she was working on her resume. She waffled on the decision; really she should stay and work on her job contacts. Lucky for us, she changed her mind, saying, "It's more important to build memories with my nephew than to work on this resume. The job search can wait, the memories won't."

I've been thinking about memories lately. It started with a comment my husband made a few weeks ago, after David's birthday party. As we were picking up the paper and ribbons he remarked, "I remember being five years old. I remember what my house looked like. I remember my friends, my brother, the things we used to do." His comments kind of brought me up short. You mean, my son could be remembering and recording the things we say and do, even at this young age? I can't remember being five years old, at least I don't think I can, not in any conscious way, but of course my subconscious mind must remember it well. And that's what's so scary about this job of parenting, at least for me. The things my son and daughter are experiencing right now are being recorded in their little brains. It's either going to be stored up on the top, ready for retrieval at any minute, or it will be stored down below, only to be retrieved on the therapist's couch. See what I mean by scary? Makes me want to quit yelling and nagging for the rest of my life, to give up all the "bad mom" things I find myself doing. If only I could.

But here's the good news about all this memory stuff. We can help create good memories for our kids. It seems we do it all the time without even knowing. At the zoo yesterday my son explained the anatomy of the orangutan's hands and feet; what it is that makes him such an agile climber. I asked him how he knew that, and he told me he learned it at a class he and I took there a few years ago. I had thought the class was a real dud; I barely remembered it. Obviously, it stuck with my son.

On the other hand, really special things I plan for my children are often forgotten. It seems going to a flower show is a lot more memorable to a forty-year-old mom than a five-year-old kid. I think it must be the incidental things kids remember, like the time I let them run up and down the moving sidewalk at the airport, or the funny way I talked at the dinner table last night.

So, here's what I know. Our kids do remember things. They remember specific things. They remember the not-so-specific things. I think they remember a general feeling of love and safety and security. I'd like to think they remember being in a place where their parents loved each other deeply, and loved them even more. If along the way they remember an orangutan class, well, that's just icing on the cake. And if they remember that I lost my temper during bath time, well, that's the stuff I hope is forgiven, if it can't be forgotten.

This morning my son and I woke to snow falling. Huge flakes floated down, covering the swing set and the bushes. I needed to get my son dressed for school. I needed to get to the post office. I decided instead to build a memory. I held my son in my lap and we looked out the window. If he won't remember this, I know I will. My memories are still building, even at this relatively old age.

My sister is right. The resume can wait. The post office can wait. Our memories can't.

MY LIFE AS A SINGLE MOM

OK, we did it again. My kids and I watched *Scooby-Doo* while eating toaster waffles and applesauce for supper. I know I should have made them pick up their toys, but what the heck, there's always tomorrow. They ask for ice cream sandwiches before bed, and I'm just too dog-tired to say no. Don't want to take a bath tonight? Fine, just so you go to bed, and Mom can have forty-five minutes of blessed peace before she flops down on her own unmade bed.

This is the way my life goes when my husband is out of town. That's when I get to play at being a single mom. But let me tell you, it is no play. It is constant— constant work, constant pleas for attention, constant activity juggling. And constant exhaustion. When the moment comes that the kids are finally asleep, I am free to do what I've been wanting to do all day. Only by then, I am too tired to remember what it was. I watch some show on TV, even though I've never watched it before and have no idea who these people are. I don't care. At least they aren't asking me to get them a drink of water, or a blanket for their fort, or to set up the swimming pool for the billionth time.

Now, I'll be honest here and say it isn't all bad. For an introvert like me, a few hours alone are wonderfully delicious, even if they are spent in mindless pursuits. And every mom who has a husband that travels will tell you the best treat of all: you don't have to cook! Because kids love grilled cheese, chicken nuggets, and waffles, and when Dad is gone, Mom is more than willing to indulge.

Still, I can't help thinking about real single mothers. The ones who don't get to see a light at the end of the week when Daddy comes home, and Mommy goes out for coffee.

Once when my husband went out of town, my neighbor asked if she could take care of my kids for a few hours while I got some errands done. And I am not lying when I say I almost got down on my knees and wept. The thought that someone would take these children for an hour while I ran to the drugstore was a precious gift from the heart.

So the next time I see a single mom, I hope I will hearken back to that feeling—the feeling of exhausted relief when I ask if I might take her kids off her hands for a few hours. Just so she can run an errand. Or sit and read the newspaper. Or just watch TV—anything but *Scooby-Doo*.

HOW HARD CAN IT BE?

It was with great pride that I took my turn this year as the Girl Scout cookie mom. Now, if you're groaning or reaching for the Rolaids, then I know that you too have been a Girl Scout cookie mom or you're married to (or were married to—I'm sure Girl Scout cookies have broken up a few solid marriages along the way) or have been the child of a Girl Scout cookie mom. Those who had been there before warned me away. I paid no heed. After all, how hard could it be? Famous last words.

The job begins by collecting the orders from the girls in the troop, adding up the numbers, and then placing the orders. So far, so good. I smirk; what's the big deal? I guess those who cautioned me away from this job just don't have the great organizational mind that I do.

A few weeks later, I go to pick up the cases of cookies at the cookie coordinator's house. She has her husband wheeling around a hand truck stacked with cases of Samoas and Thin Mints. He looks tired. She looks happy. I ask her how long she's been doing this. She says this is her ninth year. When I express my amazement, she says she's happy to do it, loves being a Girl Scout cookie mom. She says it is the one thing she does where the numbers always turn out at the end. I smile knowingly. No messy loose ends. Just like I'd like my life to be.

After getting all 1,500 boxes of these cookies crammed into my van and then onto my porch, and divvying up the boxes to the little Scouts, a problem arises. I am left with eight extra cases. Eight cases of Olé-Olés. Never heard of them? That's because no one orders them. Does "low-fat" tell you anything? No wonder they've been discontinued. Yes, I have over-ordered ninety-six boxes of these dusty little rocks.

Now here is where I'm left feeling like the Little Red Hen. "Who will help me get rid of these things?"

"Not I," said the Girl Scout office.

"Not I," said the cookie coordinator.

"Not I," said all my fellow Girl Scout moms.

"Not I," said the principal at my school.

"Not I," said every other cookie mom in the metro area.

"Not I," said all my soon-to-be ex-friends.

It turns out that I am responsible for selling these things myself. No wonder I'm a crazy woman running around with a box of cookies in each hand. The talk of cookies permeates my every conversation. I'm certain that when people see me coming, they walk to the other side of the street.

Finally, I decide to make it a family affair. I sit down with my husband and tell him he will have to set up shop at the office. "Just set a couple of piles of cookies at the corner of your desk, with a little 'For Sale' sign." My friend Debbie says that you could set out frosted doggy biscuits in an office, and within an hour they'd be gone. I figure she's right—seems people will eat anything at work, including low-fat rocks covered in powdered sugar, even if they do have to pay three dollars for the pleasure. My husband balks until I show him the math. Here is what we owe the Girl Scouts for all these cookies: $288. It's just the motivation he needs.

He becomes Cookie Dad of the Year, hawking these unwanted little rejects at every opportunity. People stop coming by to ask him questions. Meetings are cancelled, for fear he will haul out yet another plate of these delicious little treasures. Despite all this, the "frosted doggy biscuits" theory holds true. He sells all ninety-six boxes in three days.

So now, the numbers have worked out, just as the cookie coordinator said they would. I have deposited all the money, including the extra $288 windfall. My family has taken to eating Pop-Tarts and cereal for snacks. "Cookies and milk" just doesn't have the same appeal that it used to. I'm even working on repairing some of my damaged friendships.

No more messy loose ends. Just like I'd like my life to be.

MY LIFE IS A MESS

OK, I've given in. I've put in a call to the "Clutter Cutter." I did not invent this name. The person who claims this title put up her sign at a coffee shop. I tore off one of those little scraps of paper hanging like fringe from the bottom of it. This person, named Judy, guarantees she will organize my mess. I wish her luck. In fact, everyone in my immediate and extended family wishes her luck.

I don't get it. I'm really an organized person. Believe it or not, I have two calendars that I cross-reference frequently, I have a list of things to do (that I actually make use of), and I even have weekly goals for my work and home life. I've had my yearly physical, mammogram, and dental checks. My kids are all caught up on immunizations and shoes that fit. So how come I can organize my time, but not my house?

The organizational system in my house can be summed up in one word: *piles.* Let me name the piles for you just so you can see how organized I really am: "work stuff," "bills," "family stuff," "important papers," "stuff for my husband to go through," a weekly pile of "stuff that comes home every day," "stuff the kids made that I want to keep forever"… this list of piles is in fact endless. You're probably getting an image of a solitary person sitting at her keyboard surrounded by paper towers. When they find me buried in permission slips, business cards, and my lists of things to do, they'll say, "Well, at least the piles were in good order."

So, what's the big deal? Why can't I live with this organized mess? The truth is it just plain makes me crabby. I hate how it looks, and I hate how it feels. I can't find a darn thing. I estimate I use up to two hours a day just rifling through mounds of saved things. "Gotta find that free movie ticket, I know it's in there somewhere. Must be between the Sunday paper from two weeks ago, and the bill from the electric company."

Not too long ago my parents said to me, "Did you know that when you were a child you were very neat?" Now let me tell you, it's a very weird feeling to have people reveal things about you that you were never aware of—like the fact that I *used* to be neat. That I lived an uncluttered life! I imagine this sweet little girl organizing her room daily: "Let's see, spelling words will be posted here, book club order needs to go in the 'in' basket, birthday party thank-yous in the top drawer, so I can get those out by next Tuesday." I can imagine it, but let me tell you, I can't picture that that kid was me. I must have had a stand-in for those times my parents inspected my room. Just what happened along the way? At what point did I fall from a life of order and neatness? And, how can I reclaim that "inner child"? I've been trying to find her for the sake of mental and spiritual growth, but now I want to claim her so she can clean up my mess!

Instead of finding that lost neat child, I will hire Judy. She will come in and make my life (and my house) sweet and manageable, right? If nothing else, she can help me find where I left the dog.

Wish me luck.

THE TEMPTATIONS OF
CHILDHOOD

"Mom, I have something to show you." The grim words match a somber expression. A slight look of panic around the eyes nearly gives him away. My son has something to show me all right, and it isn't necessarily his latest Lego project. In case I have any doubts, I take one look at his playmate, Caroline, standing ramrod straight, arms at her side, eyes nearly twice their size. We're dealing with a major infraction here, folks.

As we're traipsing upstairs, David reminds me, "It was an accident, Mom." Well, at least it was an accident. No need for remorse or punishment.

He walks me to the closet. There on the floor is a pile of Mom's clothes. The ones that, five minutes ago, were hanging up on the metal rod across the closet—that same metal rod which is now bent nearly perfectly in half, looking like an oversized bobby pin. Seems my son was "accidentally" swinging on the rod and it "accidentally" bent in half, "accidentally" spewing my clothes all over the floor.

I am speechless, taking the time to assess the situation and gauge what should be the proper parental response to this crime. I think his friend might be holding her breath. David half smiles, half furrows his brow. Not sure which way Mom is going to move on this, he is prepared. If she decides to get angry, he's got the serious look forming. If by some miraculous act of the gods, she laughs, well, he is ready to join right in.

As it turns out, the smile is the weapon of choice. I can't help but smile. Because I can see it. I can see my son swinging from the bar. I can see it crashing. I can hear the game plan forming as he and his pal say, "Uh-oh," and decide what they're going to do next.

The temptations of childhood are many. Metal bars beg us to hang, buttons beg to be pushed, cords are there to be tugged on, and icky things are meant to be picked up, eaten, or stepped on. The sirens call out to young ears, and the only way kids can resist is if their parents tie them down or keep them busy doing chores or homework. The best a kid can hope for is that the crime be classified "accidental," so the retribution is minimal.

Somewhere along the line we learn to resist, mostly. And it's a good thing, too. Can you imagine the number of curtain rods, fire extinguishers, and table lamps we'd have to buy each year if we hadn't somehow gotten ourselves under control?

Today as I was flinging clothes from my closet floor on to my bed, I told my husband John that I understood David's temptation to swing on the closet rod. When I was a kid, I tried hanging on the chandelier in our family room. Down it came with a crash, with me attached. John was open-mouthed and speechless at the thought of his wife swinging from the ceiling.

I guess we all have skeletons in our closets; closets filled with fallen chandeliers, broken tree branches, bent curtain rods, and anything else begging to pull us off the path of goodness. And all we can do is smile, remembering how they were declared accidents.

THIS YEAR'S BIRTHDAY PARTY

My son is about to celebrate his sixth birthday, and we all know what that means: a party. I have found that just by uttering the words "birthday party" to another parent, I will get one of two very distinct and opposite reactions.

The first group is exemplified by my oh-so-enthusiastic friend, Julie. When I told her that my son's birthday was coming up, she smiled and got all excited, just like a little kid. First she wanted to know the theme of the party. "Pirates"? "Star Wars"? "Lord of the Rings"? She started spouting ideas for games like Pin the Tail on the Donkey, a treasure hunt, relay races, musical chairs. Then she moved on to the matching decorations and custom-made cake. When confronted with this type of zeal, I have found that the best course of action is to smile, perhaps through clenched teeth, and let these enthusiastic party-givers get all this gusto out of their systems. It will take a while, because they read party planning books, plan treasure hunts, and construct piñatas in their spare time.

The other camp, of which I am a charter member, will groan when I utter the words "birthday party." We cling to each other in our misery, while visions of out-of-control kids, popping balloons, and sticky chocolate frosting fill our minds. And to think, we have to have fun while we're spinning a kid around with a donkey tail (and a sharp pin!) in his hand.

Last year, I decided to face the dread and anxiety head on. With two children, I figured I had approximately twenty-five birthday parties to plan for in my future, and perhaps I needed to look at why I detested this planning. I came to a shocking realization. The truth was, I felt so darned inadequate. I mean, what if the treasure hunt was a dud? What if the kids said, "We already played this game, it's boring"? What if they went home and told their parents what a dull party it was, and how crabby the mom was, and how they never wanted to go to that crabby mom's house again, and how they didn't want to be friends with those children anymore, and what if then my children were banished from the playground, without any friends until they moved away to go to college? Whew.

Even after this painful reflection, I pushed these anxieties aside and did what had to be done. I went all out: I had a dinosaur party for my five-year-old son. You should have seen it—the dinosaur eggs, dinosaur bingo, pin the tail on the dinosaur. Halfway through the party I asked David if he was having fun. His response: "This is OK, but I didn't really want to play all these games. I just want to open presents." And so my baby got to the crux of it. Why do kids like birthday parties? For the loot. The cake, the candy, the party bags, and the presents. The games are just a sidebar on the way to the real reason we are here: the presents and the treats.

So, maybe this year I can have a new attitude while planning my son's party. I can stay unperturbed, even if I don't actually have fun watching a kid swing a bat around other kids' heads while trying to hit the piñata. I've got plenty of candy, prizes, and balloons to keep everyone satisfied.

Besides, after a few years this party stuff will all be over. Then we'll move on to teenage sleepovers…

Suddenly the idea of a treasure hunt sounds mighty appealing. I better get planning.

AN ENTERTAINING THEORY

I was having a good day. Just walking around, minding my own business, feeling fine about life in general. But then I got the dreaded phone call: my cheerful spouse announcing that he was bringing the boss and "a few of the gang" over for appetizers and drinks before their big annual dinner. "So, honey," he intoned, already sensing my panic, "all we have to do is put together a few appetizers." (This was followed by silence. Painful silence.) He continued, "Just put out some cheese and crackers and peanuts." Sure. Like I was going to serve bar food to my husband's boss and coworkers.

Now, my mother loves to entertain. I was surprised when she and my dad bought a larger condo last year. The reason she gave: *she needed more room so that she could fit more friends into her house.* I, on the other hand, still have to call her *every* time I have company over: "Quick, Mom, a recipe that's easy and serves twelve." "How about a dish to serve the new neighbors?" This walking, talking recipe book calls me back in minutes with step-by-step instructions.

This time, because my mom was out of town, I had to turn to my fallback position: phone a friend. Someone for whom "hors d'oeuvre" was not a dirty word.

I quickly called my friend Joan, who knows how to do *everything*, including how to keep a perfect house and lawn and make perfect appetizers, all while working on her PhD. She calmed me down and assured me that she had the perfect recipe: goat cheese torte. Here's what gives it its claim to perfection: a) it is made with exotic-sounding ingredients like goat cheese and basil and sun-dried tomatoes, b) these ingredients are available at your local grocery store, and c) it's so easy, even *you* can make it.

I did make it, and it was quite a sight to behold. I polished off the dusty dishes, bought some real nice crackers, and set out the goat cheese torte. Everyone was impressed. I squeaked by again.

A few days later, I asked Joan where she had learned all her tricks. How is she able to summon a recipe from her arsenal without breaking into a cold sweat? She told me she has a theory. She believes that skills such as cooking and cleaning skip a generation. She uses her own family as an example. When she was growing up, her mom's goal was to do the least amount of housework necessary so that she could get to the next novel calling to her from her nightstand. While the dust bunnies gathered, and the instant soup overflowed, she had her nose firmly planted in a Jacqueline Susann novel. Joan has made up for her mother's flaws in spades.

I, on the other hand, spent my childhood waking to the sound of the vacuum cleaner running and the smell of spaghetti sauce cooking on the stove. Proving Joan's theory correct, I must say I find the vacuum just a little too cumbersome to push around, and I have learned to believe that spaghetti sauce in a jar really does taste pretty darn close to homemade.

To take her theory one step further, I look to my children, the next generation. And I must say, they had better get going. If the clothes and toys scattered across their floors are any indication, they have a lot to learn.

When I try to "teach" them to cook, enthusiastically mixing up a batch of instant pancake mix with them, their little eyes soon glaze over, and they say, "This is fun, Mom, but I really have some math tables to memorize. Call me when they're done."

Maybe I can't push this theory. Perhaps it's all genetic, and their entertaining/cleaning/cooking gene will present itself when the time is right. I really do hope so.

In the meantime, I've got my book club group coming over for dessert. I've already put a call in to my mom.

THE CHOICES WE MAKE

My six-year-old son is in a "stage." We have been parents long enough to know that this is a stage, and not a permanent personality defect, thank God. You see, when given the choice between two really great 'kid' things, say, going swimming or going fishing, he cries. He weeps and blubbers and says, "I can't choose. I know I'll be sorry if I miss the other thing." Finally, with lots of counseling and encouragement and occasional threats on our part ("Make a choice now, or they'll leave without you!"), he makes a choice. Then the crying starts all over. A kind of grieving for the thing he will be missing. Then he says, "OK, this hurts too much, I'll choose the other thing." Oh, but then the water wells up again—sadness over losing that first choice, which may have been a lot more fun than the second choice in the end. On and on it goes. Finally, his father or I take over and tell him *we'll* decide. We even go so far as to take one of the choices away by telling a little white lie: "You know, I just heard the pool is closed, so swimming really isn't an option anyway." Anything to get this kid over his grief and on to the fun of childhood.

I know how he feels. My good choices in life are many. On days when I've got lots of time stretched in front of me, I ask, "Should I write this story about my son, should I prepare a talk to that mothers' group, or should I go to the print shop and have new business cards made?" Then there are the big choices: "Should I accept that job, even if it has lower pay but supposedly better opportunities for the future, or should I stay where I'm comfortable but just a little bored?" The choices are too many, and I want to weep. What if I pick the wrong one? What if that missed opportunity is the one thing that would have made a difference in my life, would have changed everything? I'll never know, that's for sure. And it's the not knowing that keeps me immobilized. So, like my son, I howl and blubber and fail to make a decision.

I told a friend about this problem with my son. She replied that she too knew exactly how he felt. "I hate having too many good choices. I go to the State Fair every year, and then it comes time to choose what I'll eat. Should I go with a corn dog, or branch out to deep-fried candy bars? Stick with the malts at the dairy barn, or move on to root beer at the stand on the corner? Finally I go back to the same food choices I always make." She told me this story with a kind of sadness, a wistfulness for opportunities lost. What was she missing by taking the same old route? On the other hand, how does she overcome the fear and sadness of giving up what she knows and loves?

I turn to my husband, who is flipping a coin to help him decide what shirt to wear to work. Yes, even little choices can be difficult.

So maybe this isn't a stage with my son. Maybe he will always need to grieve the thing given up. Or maybe he'll never know what he missed. Perhaps he can convince himself that opportunities are not lost forever. The chance to go swimming will surely come along another day. Maybe. No wonder we're all crying over these choices. We just don't know.

I counsel my friend and myself just as I counsel my son. Go ahead, take a chance. Make a choice. Everyone says that there are really no wrong decisions, just different decisions that will take you down a different path. And if you do miss an extraordinary opportunity, it will probably come along later in life.

If I fail to convince her or fail to convince myself, I tell a little white lie, just as I've told my son. I tell myself that the TV show is no longer available, so it never was a choice. Or I suggest that it's surely going to rain, so I can't go biking anyway. It's a lie, a hoax. But it gets me over the weeping, the second-guessing, the grieving for that imagined lost opportunity. And just as I tell my son, I need to take a risk and make my choice now, or they'll surely leave without me. And good choice or not, I would never want them to leave without me.

IT TAKES A VILLAGE

(to Raise a Softball Player)

The crowning moment came at second base. There stood my daughter, and the ball was coming right at her! A slow motion arc to her little outstretched glove. Looks of painful pessimism ("Here we go again") passed between my husband and me, right as that big beautiful softball landed smack dab in the center of her mitt. Christine looked at her hand as if it were attached to someone else, but it was true—the ball was there, her foot was on the base, and the runner was out! Her dad and I held on to each other for support, lest we fall backwards off the bleachers. We exchanged a nervous laugh, some reassurance that we had actually seen what we had seen, and then muttered words of "I knew she could do it."

As she ran off the field, my daughter said to me, "Coach Bob says that was the best play he's seen me make in two years." Indeed.

A little background: when it comes to softball, my husband and I are what you might call clueless. We just don't know much about how the game is played.

At the beginning of the season, I encouraged my husband to practice with Christine. So he dutifully bought a ball, pulled out an old hand-me-down-mitt, and practiced. He threw; she attempted to hit. The sole coaching tip I heard him give her was "Keep your eye on the ball." I asked if perhaps he could give her any more suggestions, and his response was, "That's the only thing my dad told me when I was little." And I had to admit that was the only thing I had heard too. See what I mean? Clueless.

I knew it was time for drastic action. I needed to find someone with a larger arsenal of advice than we had to offer. I decided to bribe our minister. He was the obvious choice because: a) he knew how to play softball, b) he was single and childless, thereby giving him unlimited time to work with my daughter (after he got the sermon written, of course), and c) he didn't know how to cook. I invited him to supper. After a large satisfying meal, I *casually* mentioned that my daughter was just starting softball, and would he like to go out and "throw the ball around"? (This was a phrase I had heard other people use.) He agreed, and I knew I had him. Turns out guys like him can't stand to see someone who doesn't know how to play ball. He spent hours out in the backyard showing my daughter how to position her glove for catching the ball, and how to hit the ball, while I dutifully took notes on the things he was saying.

Next, I enlisted the aid of my children's babysitter, a member of the local high school's softball team. A casual mention of softball season sent her scrambling to the backyard, bat and ball in hand. I can still see her throwing the ball to my daughter, using Christine's little brother as a fielder, while we, the parents, happily drove off to the movies.

So, there stood my little girl. After two years of advice from Pastor Peter, two years of the babysitter fielding balls in the backyard, and two years of coaches working with her endlessly, pulling her elbow up here, giving her words of praise there, even wiping away tears of discouragement, my daughter was standing on second base with the ball in her hand. And the runner was out. Gosh, I love sports.

This year my son is starting soccer. I've heard that the neighbor across the street knows how to play. I hope she'll accept my invitation to dinner.

A TRULY GIFTED SEAMSTRESS

There was a time when my husband believed I could be a seamstress. We were young, newly married, and open to possibilities. One day I came home from my very first job to our very first apartment, and John told me he had a surprise for me. "Sit here on the chair and close your eyes... Now, listen." Soon I heard the familiar whirr of a sewing machine. I opened my eyes to see my husband bending over a piece of fabric as he operated a very big, very old Sears and Roebuck sewing machine. John smiled proudly, "I remember you said you would like to start sewing, so I bought this for you. It's used, but it seems to work just fine." His joy at helping me fulfill my dream (even though I couldn't really remember expressing a passion for sewing) made me want to jump in and try. Unfortunately, eager enthusiasm for a new skill did not translate to beautiful clothing. The dresses and shirts I so lovingly stitched together looked like they had been made in my seventh-grade home economics class, which was in fact the last place I had sewn anything. I reluctantly stowed the machine in the back of a closet.

A few years later my sewing skills were given a renewed opportunity. We had just bought a new house, and we could see the windows needed something to soften the harsh look of the rickety shades. I made a trip to the fabric store, and explained our decorating dilemma. The clerk asked, "Can you sew a straight seam?," to which I could confidently respond in the affirmative. "Well," she said, "then you can make curtains." And she showed me how. She told me which curtain rods to buy, how much fabric to buy, and where to sew the seams. I went home and did as she told me, and the final product really was quite stunning. Stunning because it looked so nice, and stunning because it had come from my hands, the hands of a seamstress. I decided then and there that my husband's faith in my sewing skills was not misplaced.

Soon I moved on to making different types of curtains (simple, always simple), for the other windows in the house, even little curtains for the basement and garage windows. My antique machine and I just kept plowing away on those straight seams.

Alas, we moved away from that house a few years later, and I was sad to leave my little creations behind. It was clear that our new home, with its state-of-the-art shades and draperies would no longer require the services of this talented little seamstress and her big ole machine. Once again, the sewing machine was tucked away in a closet.

Until this year. We replaced the house's original windows with brand-new ones. And those windows really needed something to dress them up. My seamstress instincts were kicking in, and soon I had lugged out the old lady and set her up on the kitchen table. I went to the fabric store and picked out some bright yellow fabric for my daughter's windows. Another sweet clerk helped me measure how much fabric to buy, and showed me once again where to sew the seams.

Away I went, hunched over the needle, foot pressing down, gears spinning. And again, I created an impressive showpiece, if I do say so myself, which I do, again and again, to anyone who visits our house. "Want to see my daughter's new curtains?" My friends, being the well-trained pals that they are, are dutifully impressed. "Where did you get those?," they'll ask.

"Oh," I say, with a nonchalant wave of hand, "I made them over the weekend."

Yes, young love was right. I am a seamstress, and I have the curtains to prove it. Thank goodness this house gives me myriad opportunities to show off my skill. It's amazing how many windows one house has.

And who knows? Maybe once all the windows are done, I'll move on to pillow covers, or dishcloths. The old machine is out and waiting, and this seamstress is ready for her next home project.

THE MOST WONDERFUL
TIME OF THE YEAR

I just got off the phone with my friend Joan. "You know," she says, "if I have to fill one more water balloon, I'll lose my mind. I just can't do summer anymore." I imagine her talking to me with the phone tucked between her head and shoulder, sweat running down her brow, as she stretches yet one more balloon across the tap. Her boys smile as she hands them another bucketful of water bombs.

I am afraid that many of us share her feelings. Yes, the bright appeal of summer has started to lose its shine. And right about now we're just letting ourselves imagine the beautiful sounds of the school bell ringing, beckoning our children to get out of their wet shorts and sandals, to finish up that last sticky Popsicle, and brush the sand off the car seat. It's time to go to school.

Don't get me wrong: I love summer. There is nothing so sweet as that last day of school when the kids come home, empty the contents of their backpacks into the trash, and put on their swimsuits. The lovely anticipation of days at the beach, biking on trails, and lazing around with friends is well founded. It's just that after about the middle of July, what was once beautiful becomes a beast. Suddenly, a trip to the beach means wet sand on the floor. A trip to the playground means one more ride with eight of your children's closest friends in a hot van with sticky seats. Or, as Joan discovered, water balloons become just one more chore on the list of things to do. Drudgery sets in. Not to mention boredom. We start to mutter phrases our mothers once said: "I'm not your entertainment director!" or "If you're bored, go ride your bike around the block!" or better yet, "If you're bored, I'll be happy to give you something to do!," which of course means scrubbing the kitchen floor or organizing the toys in the garage.

A few years ago, a commercial aired on television which captured the feeling perfectly. The dad is "back-to-school" shopping with his children. The kids are walking with heads bowed, arms at their sides, and pathetically sad faces. Meanwhile, the dad has a huge triumphant grin on his face, one foot on the cart, the other foot kicked up behind him as he sails down the aisle. The song "It's the Most Wonderful Time of the Year" plays.

Most of us share his exuberance. It's time to get back to the blessed structure that school brings to our days. Yet, having been children once ourselves, we can relate to how our kids must feel. Their days of freedom are numbered, and they know it.

I need to muster a little empathy here, and find a way to ease their transition from the languid days of vacation to the rigorous routine of school. In some ways, I think my kids look forward to starting the school year too, although they would probably never admit it. Maybe with a little cajoling, they too can see back-to-school as the most wonderful time of the year, which indeed it most certainly is.

THE OTHER SIDE OF THE PAGE

Last week my son invited me to visit his first-grade class. I imagine that all over the country children proudly show off their spelling tests and newly solved math problems to their parents with some regularity. But it's different for my son. For him, school is just an interruption in his train of thought. He's thinking about what causes the hands of a clock to move, when suddenly his teacher is asking him to write the alphabet. He is engaged in a secret war between the earthlings and the aliens, and his fantasy is interrupted by "Turn in your math papers now."

"Math papers? We were working on math?" School is a burden for this young dreamer, I'm afraid.

So imagine my surprise and joy when this little thinker invited me to visit his school—he had something to show me. I arrived at the end of the school day. He pulled out the paper—a superhero colored in with blue, red, and yellow crayon. I realized his source of pleasure—this superhero was not only cool, it was actually an assignment—imagine being *told* to draw a superhero. At this point, the teacher jumped into the act: "Would you like to show your mom your writing folder?" A quick imperceptible roll of the eyes, told me that, actually, he would rather not, but who's gonna say no to the teacher?

After much digging through two weeks of accumulated (and unfinished) papers, he extracted the folder. The first (and only) page said "I see a blue ocean." Hardly the type of phrase that would pop out of this child's mouth. He said, "The teacher told us to write that." Then, turning ever so slightly, so as to exclude the hovering teacher, he whispered, "Look what I made on the back." On the back of the stilted sentence, he had drawn a tiny picture. He said, "This is an octopus, and these are the tentacles. One has zoomed off, and is a rocket ship. It's landing on the moon." Excitement and joy filled his face. On one side of the page, along with the formal assigned sentence, was the blue ocean, drawn in perfectly measured waves. On the other side, well, fantasy, fun, and joy.

I've been thinking about this lately, this little war that occurs in my son's daily life; his internal need to create, to dream, and to imagine versus the external need to learn the tools that will help him succeed. He needs to learn to read, to add up the numbers, to follow the rules. Trying to help him balance the internal with the external will be a constant struggle.

Our children have a lot to tell us. My son tells me, go ahead, do what you're supposed to do: color inside the lines, and put the capitals and periods in all the right places. But when you're done, don't be afraid to turn the page over and draw an octopus floating to the moon, or wherever else your imagination takes you. That's where the real joy lies.

CLEANING UP MY MESS

A few months ago, I did the unthinkable: I fired my cleaning lady. And now, like an errant child with her head bowed, I was dialing her phone number. Trying to sound cheerful, my voice was soon cracking... would she consider coming back?

For years Gladys had toiled over my messy bathrooms, dusty cupboards, and coffee-stained sinks. She worked with an efficiency I truly never appreciated. In fact, I so underestimated her skills that, like a cocky teenager, I told myself, "I can do that." And now, after two months of trying, that cocky teenager was saying, "Yeah, right." Never again. I'm writing all this down so in those times of fogginess when I think I might get rid of the cleaning lady, someone can wave this essay under my nose and say, "Don't do it! Remember what happened the last time you fired her!"

My sorry days without Gladys were spent lugging a vacuum cleaner up the stairs while hoses and nozzles dropped like leaves off a tree. I was stuck reading the labels of various cleaning solutions, trying to figure out which product got sprayed where and for what reason. I shed my clothes as I sprayed and scrubbed the cloudy buildup on the shower door. My dog barked incessantly as I waved the feather duster over the shelves; he wanted to catch that flying bird, and the crazy woman who was chasing it around. By the time my kids came home from school their mother was a sweaty, chlorine-scented wild woman. "No, I can't help you with your homework! I've got one more sink to clean!"

So, with rubber gloves in hand I decided to make, pardon the pun, a clean sweep of it. I called Gladys. She left me hanging for a painful moment while she consulted her calendar. "Yes. There might just be an opening… today."

I threw my dust cloth in the air with joy. "When can you come?"

"Well…" (I could see the power building in her.) "I just don't know, but hang around; we'll be there." All appointments were cancelled as I waited by the window for Gladys' arrival.

I tried to remain neutral when I told her my cleaning problems. But soon it was spilling out in a torrent of lament: "I can't get the sink clean, I can't get that crud off the shower door, the kitchen floor is sticky all the time…"

She shook her head and smiled. And, with a voice reserved for a disobedient child who needs forgiveness, she said, "Of course you don't know how to do that. That's why we do it for you." And she set to work. First she pulled out the rubber gloves that had melted into one big ball. "These," she said, in a tone which was perfectly matched by her quick, efficient movements, "these gloves are like this because you didn't rinse your hands after cleaning the toilet. The solution melted the gloves." I nodded and took mental notes. "Now," she asked, "where is the stainless cleaner?" I rifled through various bottles and cans, finding what looked like the right scouring powder. I never did find it. No matter, she knew what to use instead.

Yes, Gladys is back, and I am oh-so-glad. And I think I've learned a thing or two. First, cleaning is a skill, at least if you want it done right. As Gladys told me, there are people who specialize in cleaning; they are good at it, and "you are not." Second (and don't we all know this?), you don't know what you've got 'til it's gone.

I love my clean house, and I love Gladys. She's mine. I appreciate her. And believe me, I'll never let her go.

THE SCARIEST DAY OF ALL

Halloween is coming, and it's giving me the creeps. I'm nervous, I'm shaking, and I'm downright full of anxiety over this day. Is it the thought of the living dead making their appearance at my doorstep? Perhaps the sight of blood has me queasy. No, it starts with something a whole lot scarier: costumes. As in my children's costumes.

You see, folks, Halloween taps right into my little voice of inadequacy. The voice that assures me I just do not have a creative bone in my body. When my daughter comes home and says she wants to be a robot, I start running, panic coursing through my mind. Let's see, a box. I need a big box, silver spray paint. After spending hours taping boxes together with duct tape and string, or applying all shades of gray to my child's beaming face, I take a look at my completed creation. What do I see? A child wearing a taped together box, two crooked wires popping out of her headband, and a smear of silver across her nose. The doorbell rings: it is my daughter's best friend. She is dressed as Princess Leia: white gown flowing, hair perfectly coiled around her ears. I hate this girl's mother. I didn't used to hate her, but tonight I do, as my kid stands there looking like some strange intergalactic orphan, and her friend is looking like Carrie Fisher dropped in from Hollywood. Strangely, my daughter seems not to notice. It's the one opportunity to walk around looking goofy, and believe me, she certainly does. Not to mention the fact that in a few short hours she will be bringing home a sack full of candy.

Let's talk about this Halloween booty. Don't get me wrong: I don't hate candy, in moderation. But every year I get overwhelmed by the sheer volume of sugar coursing through my house. A few years ago I devised a plan. Appealing to their sense of charity, I told my kids that we should give half their candy to "poor" people. It worked! I won't say they went so far as to give up their most choice pieces, but they did hand over a bag full of peanut butter chews and coconut patties. Then last year, my son had a thought. "Hey, if poor people need candy, why don't they just go trick-or-treating themselves?" A light bulb went off in his head. He'd been duped. No more "candy for the poor" at our house. No, we get to keep all this sweetness for ourselves, and it lasts all the way to Valentine's Day, when we are deluged with chocolate and cherry gumdrops.

So, here I am, faced with a holiday that leaves me feeling nervous and inadequate and makes my teeth ache. My friends tell me to relax and enjoy the holiday. After all, it makes our children so happy. Riding on a roller coaster makes my children happy too, and you don't see me doing that, do you?

Last night I went to a meeting at my kids' school to plan the annual Halloween party. I actually got assigned to the haunted house committee. I was careful not to tell the group how much October 31st gives me the heebie-jeebies. Soon after, my friend Jenny called to tell me she had seen me at the meeting, and in her words, "Your neck looked stiff." Hmm, guess you can't fool everyone, no matter how hard you try.

My kids think Halloween ranks right up there with their birthdays and Christmas. So, I'll keep trying. I'll smile when I assemble my son's devil costume. Grit my teeth when my children consume *one more* Butterfinger before dinnertime, and show enthusiasm as I pound that last nail into the coffin at school. Yes, for the sake of my children, I can keep smiling, even if it does give me the creeps… and a stiff neck.

SPEECHLESS

I have not spoken for three days.

Once a year, Mother Nature has her way with my vocal cords, holding my throat in a grip of silence called laryngitis, and I am rendered speechless.

What happens when you go to bed chatting and wake up completely silent is remarkable. My muted state has sent shock waves through my family's system.

At first, my children seem to take no notice, yammering on with their stories and their questions. They are caught off guard by my lack of response. They become little clowns, making faces, using silly voices. When they are met with silent laughter or a smile, they move away. This was not the audience they had hoped for.

My husband is afraid I am giving him the silent treatment. He knows it's not true, yet seems to need reassurance. He looks at me and whispers (whispers seem to beget whispers), "Are you mad at me, or something?" (echoes of nervous phrases we used with each other in high school).

Even the dog has spun ever so slightly out of control. With no master to yell "NO" when he chews on my children's shoes, he has been banished to his kennel. Turns out my voice is the only one he'll obey.

But the ripples this silence has sent through my family is nothing compared to the damage it is doing to my psyche. Yesterday, my husband looked at me and said, "Right now you are sitting and thinking about how awful your life is, aren't you?" He was right of course. After twenty-one years of marriage, he recognizes that vaguely anxious look.

Inside this igloo of isolation, I have come to realize that these thoughts born in my brain need a way out. Like a pent-up sneeze, these little droplets need to escape now, lest they back up and cause infection. Fretful questions like "Am I ever going to find the right job?," "Are my children doing well?," and "Am I a success?" become defining queries for me. Without some way to show these festering notions the door, I am left feeling a failure. My life is useless. I have squandered my purpose, sold myself short.

Now I know why I meet my friends for coffee and conversation once a week. Thoughts have a way of getting musty and dark and painful when they're bottled up. Without a good shaking out, the worst ones overtake us. And talking seems to be their only escape.

Today I sit at the coffee shop alone, with no one to talk to, because I cannot. Instead, I listen to the other coffee drinkers. Their conversations vary from trivial to crucial. But they are talking. And because of that, they can go on with their days, perhaps with clearer minds and a renewed optimism that all is well in their worlds. I plan to join them soon.

A VERY TRADITIONAL CHRISTMAS

Every year we put up our Christmas tree in the same spot. Poor tree. At our house, if you are a defenseless tree left standing out in an open space, chances are very good that you will get chewed on by the dog, bumped into by wrestling children, or become overburdened with the Legos little boys choose to hide on your branches. This year my husband and I decided to give the little tree a break, and put it up in a different spot; a more secluded corner, one where it would be free to shine and lend Christmas cheer without fear of being toppled.

It was not to be. As soon as my husband had the tree stand out of the box and assembled in the corner, my daughter's protests started: "WAIT! We can't put it there! We NEVER put it there! It's TRADITION!" And that sealed the little tree's fate. Back into the battle zone it went, because, after all, it is tradition.

My son entered the room, and soon his lip began to quiver. "Somebody put the star on top of the tree!" (His sister had.) "It's my job to do that! I do it every year! It's…" (you guessed it) "TRADITION!"

All this makes me think about the word tradition. I know I've raised an emotional brood around here, but I wonder if their needs are reflective of all of our needs, especially around the holidays. We need to hang our stockings on something we can count on, a ritual that gives us comfort and pleasure every single year. If putting the tree in that corner made me happy last year and the year before, well, I can count on it providing joy this year too.

So, along comes a new parental responsibility: building traditions. And for me, that's kind of a weighty proposition. I have to be careful. Because if an activity is done once, well, maybe I can sweep it under the rug and pretend it never happened. But if it happens twice, well, it becomes a tradition, which is sacred around here.

Among the activities to which we were happy to bid farewell: "Breakfast with Santa," which included burnt French toast and a too-long line, resulting in photos of a hysterical child sitting on an overworked Santa's lap; going caroling in subzero temperatures (never again); and making homemade gifts for everyone on our list, which resulted in many puddles of drippy wax and permanently stained counters.

Among the traditions we have built, and that I am willing to keep: shopping for needy children overseas, decorating cookies with friends (especially since we do it at their house), and shopping for family members at the "dollar store." The picture of my kids' smiles as they pick out the perfect soap dish for their grandma and extension cord for their grandpa helps me understand why the cliché "the true meaning of Christmas" was invented.

"Without our traditions, our lives would be as shaky as a fiddler on a roof!" So declares Tevye in the play of the same name. I know my children would agree with that, and I guess I would too. I'm glad they helped me see it.

DOWN AND OUT IN MINNESOTA

Thoughts occur to a person on the way down. They begin to form as one's body is making that perfect arc in the air. Feet fly up; arms open widely; up, up, up; then down, down, down with one bone-crunching thud. First: "I can't believe I'm actually falling on my butt in the middle of the street in front of my child's school. Just a few seconds ago I was walking with confidence in my stride, only to have it broken by this one patch of ice." Then, "I wonder if it is possible to break one's behind? Can they put it in a cast?" Then it's: "I wonder if that Suburban cruising past me is going to stop, pick up my shattered rag doll body and take me home?" And finally, the clincher, the one I've been thinking for oh-so-many years: "Why, oh why, do I live here?"

Now this last thought has been rattling around in my brain and out my mouth for a number of years. How did someone like me, someone who hates the cold more than anybody I know, end up living in Minnesota? Whenever I voice this, the listener invariably asks, "Where did you grow up?" I say, "Wisconsin." With a look of wonderment, the listener *always* says, "Well, you should be used to it by now." I'm telling you, there is never a variation in this conversation. For some reason, growing up with below-zero temps and shoulder-high snowbanks should endear me to this climate. It hasn't happened yet.

Well, at least I have some allies in this fight against Old Man Winter—that is, I thought I did. My parents live in Wisconsin; I have a sister in Michigan, another one in New York. They all put up with the cold, so why can't I? Imagine my surprise when my parents bought a condo in Florida. Not rented—bought. Like they're going to move there or something. Well, it started out innocently enough. They spent a few months down there. But then things started to change. Without clearing it with me, they started adding days, weeks, a month or two here and there. Next thing I knew, they were telling me they wouldn't be in Wisconsin for the holidays, but I was welcome to join them in Florida. Hmm.

Well, that was OK; I still had my sis in Upper Michigan. But before you can say "wind-chill factor" she up and moved to Colorado! I've already got two other siblings in that state with an oh-so-mild climate. Their comments are enough to set your teeth on edge: "You ought to see it. It snowed yesterday, we skied in the mountains, and now it's all melted so the kids can skateboard in the street!"

Now, I'll bet you can guess what happened next. The last remaining sibling moved to Los Angeles! As in California! I am the sole survivor. The one left in the deep freeze. And all the while I'm yelling, "Hey, I thought we were in this together! You know I hate winter more than all of you!" But they can't hear me over the sound of people splashing in the swimming pool, or their laughter as they ride their bicycles down the street.

So, as I lay there, staring into the sky, I thought of this fate of mine. How did I get to this point? This point of dragging myself to school, with tears streaming down my cheeks, "Teacher, I hurt my bottom!" (Much to my daughter's horrified embarrassment). How is it I ended up with a life where I have to call my husband home from work because my derriere is in such pain? How did I get to the place where I have to call in to my job saying I can't possibly work today because my— ahem—rear end is injured? It was the last straw. I've tried accepting, if not embracing, Old Man Winter. I think he has won.

Sitting on a hot pad (or is it an icepack?) later that day I checked my e-mails. An innocent and happy note from my parents: "Just thought you would like to know. We received our Florida license plates today. We are well on our way to become Florida residents!" I think that's called adding insult to injury. OK, I'm beat. Guess I'll just have to put on another sweater, lace on the snowshoes, and accept defeat. I'm in this frigid icebox alone. All I ask is if you seeing me lying in the middle of the street, please, oh please, pick me and take me home to bed. And put on a few extra blankets, if you will.

MORNING MADNESS

Well, the children are off to school, and I can sit down and finish my cup of coffee, maybe read the paper. But first I need to take a deep breath. I just went through another morning rush with my children, and I need some time to recover.

I thought we were doing fine. Really. The lunches were packed, the teeth were brushed, the homework was assembled. But just when things were going smoothly, the gods of disorder needed to do their work. It seems every family has to have a little sand thrown into the gears of their morning routine—something to get the mother yelling and the adrenaline flowing. My friend Cindy tells me that things at her house will be going along just fine, and then she'll look over and see her daughters playing the piano, petting the dog, or just generally lying on the floor—anything to keep from doing those mundane tasks like getting dressed and brushing teeth. The more she yells, the slower they move. My coworker, Lynne, has the daunting chore of getting a teenage boy out the door. After shaking him out of his slumber three separate times, during which she swears he has responded in a clear and audible tone, he'll eventually stumble bleary-eyed into the kitchen asking, "Why didn't you wake me up?"

The little bug in our mix today was my daughter's hair. We were doing fine… until she looked into the mirror. A tiny little errant wave had popped up on her head. She immediately begged for help. I yanked out the curling iron and proceeded to pull and cook her hair, all the while muttering, "I don't know why I do this, I don't know why I do this, we're going to be late again." Her brother knew to take his place on the couch until the smoke cleared. Turns out my amateur styling only made it worse, as a corkscrew cascaded down the top of Christine's hair. And this is when our defining morning moment occurred. Realizing that I had the wrong tool for the job, I did a sprint for the upstairs bathroom to retrieve the proper iron. The only problem was the open kitchen cupboard door that I needed to get past. This was at knee level, and darned if I didn't try to run past it instead of closing it. In my rush and extreme agitation, I tried sidestepping the door, but instead ran right into it. In what appeared to me as a slow-motion act of destruction, the cupboard door split right in two and clattered to the floor. It was like someone had taken a clean karate kick to a piece of wood. My son got off his perch long enough to see what the crash was. My daughter retreated into the bathroom. The dog came around to sniff. The silence was broken only by my son asking, "Are you all right?" And then the car pool pulled into the driveway.

Today my daughter entered the car pool with tears about to spill over (and a curl down the back of her head), my son is keeping out of mom's way, and even the dog has retreated. I'm drinking my coffee, and wondering if it's a little too early in the morning for a glass of wine.

I don't know how this happens. But happen it does and happen it will in the future. The only thing I can do is expect it. And maybe make sure the kitchen cupboards are closed before I start running.

A LIFE OF HIS OWN

Last night my son received a phone call. This is not an earth-shattering event in most homes, but then again, most homes are not ours. You see, my six-year-old son does not "do" phones. He apparently sees no reason to gab into a device that is made solely for the purpose of conversing with another person. Perhaps if it had a few bells and whistles attached, maybe a video screen, things would be different. But I think not. To him, telephones are an interruption to his day, time away from building with Legos or swinging in the backyard. His grandparents have given up. They know requests to talk to David are futile and will be met with the same response: "Uh, maybe later." But of course there is no later. No, my boy is just not one for idle conversation.

But last night someone, a young someone, called and asked for David. Knowing he would never quit playing with his Spider-Man figure long enough to put the receiver to his ear, I covered for him, and told the kid that David wasn't home. A little white lie, but why turn off potential buddies right from the get-go? The caller told me that his name was Joe, and that he and my son had talked on the playground at school today about Joe's baseball game. He was wondering if David would like to come.

When David came into the room I asked him about Joe. In a casual tone that would have me believe he is Mr. Congeniality at his school, David said, "Oh yeah, he's my friend. He invited me to his baseball game tonight. I told him we had nothing going on, and that we would probably come." Enter the older sister, my little spy, and she informs me that Joe is a fourth-grader, and she sees David playing with Joe and Phillip, another fourth-grader on the playground at recess. Turns out that Joe is actually a pretty nice kid, and the most positive recommendation of all: "He never gets in trouble at school."

"So," I ask David, "what do you and Joe do at recess?"

"Oh, we just walk around the playground and talk." Talk? His sister and I are flabbergasted. "You walk around and TALK, as in converse?" David throws open the back door and yells over his shoulder, "Yeah, I'm going back outside, see ya!"

So what happened? I gave birth to this child, fed him, diapered him, and pretty much took care of his whole young life from clothes to friends to preschool. But somewhere on the way to first grade, my boy developed a life of his own. A life where he walks around the perimeter of the playground, talking to older kids about baseball. A life over which I have little control or influence. In fact, he seems to have a personality that I don't know about, one that invites kids to call him on the phone just so he'll come watch their game.

So, we went to Joe's game. I don't know Joe, but I cheered along with the rest of 'em. David watched the game for a little bit, and then found an inviting pile of sand. After I admonished him for not watching the game, he informed me that it was boring, and that he was working on making a cool castle. Now, that's my old David—the one that can't resist the pull of an untamed pile of dirt. Friends and conversation are important, but, as he would say, "Uh, maybe later."

A WRINKLE-FREE EXISTENCE

Here is what I remember: I am an eight-year-old girl, sitting cross-legged on the braided rug in our family room. My mom has the television on; it's her favorite show: *Password*. Allen Ludden and his celebrity guests are giving one-word clues. My mother has lugged out the big creaky ironing board. She wrestles the board and it opens with a loud groaning sound. Today's chore: ironing. Fill the heavy silver beast with distilled water, spray the starch, let out a spurt of steam, and the ironing has begun. My only task as my mother steams and sweats is to run to the television set and turn down the volume as the announcer tells the viewing audience the "word." I like this feeling; I like the radiating warmth of the heavy iron; I like the soft sounds of the steam rolling out; and the smell, I love the smell. Fresh-ironed cotton shirts. My mom teaches me to iron handkerchiefs. The pure symmetry of folding the cloth in half, in half again, and finally into a perfect square is just so satisfying to my young mind. Ironing: warmth, order, good smells, celebrities laughing on the television set, and most of all, having my mother nearby.

Many years later, my mother is living in a condo in Florida. I go to visit her, and when I notice my cotton shirt is full of creases and wrinkles from having been stored in a suitcase too long, I ask her where her ironing board is. She actually has to stop and think. "Oh, that's right; it's in the closet, behind the luggage." Indeed. It is behind the luggage and the board games and the vast collection of seashells. It is clear that this woman is no longer spending her mornings with Allen Ludden and Betty White. When I ask her about this, she says, "Iron, who irons anymore?" and off she goes to her water-aerobics class.

I've polled my friends and family, and there is definitely an alarming trend here. Many people are rejecting the time-honored tradition of ironing. These people just do not iron, except in extreme emergency, like a formal dinner with the president. They simply cannot be bothered by wrinkles, and furthermore, seem to almost embrace the rumpled look. Recently, when my sister saw my creaking old monster of a board set up in the basement, she remarked, "I hate ironing so much that I will buy a new shirt before I have to iron." I believe her.

I admit that ironing can sometimes be a pain in the neck, and sometimes I put off this overwhelming chore. But when my husband comes downstairs wearing nothing but a pair of pants and a bare belly, I know it is time to attack the heap. He may suggest that he doesn't mind wearing a wrinkled shirt, or that he could iron it himself, but I want to be the one to do the ironing in our family.

I am part of a group of folks that knows the value of a good ironing session. We love the warmth of the fabric, the smell of clean shirts, and more than anything, to know that we have accomplished the goal of eradicating all wrinkles for that week. We may not have *Password* anymore, but we do have our irons, and our wrinkle-free dignity.

THE EMPEROR'S NEW GLASSES

Somewhere on my way to turning forty, it happened. The print got smaller. Or else my arms got shorter. In any case, it was inevitable. If I were going to remain a member of the literate world, I had to give in. I was getting older, and it was time to get bifocals.

I walked down to our neighborhood optical shop and introduced myself to Mo, the go-to "glasses guy." He fitted me with just the thing: very cool tortoise-shell frames which I believed looked more like a fashion statement than a geriatric aid.

When I put the new glasses on my face, I was shocked. There was a line, a very *noticeable* line going right across the middle of my eyes.

Mo assured me that he could hardly see the line. "Really, only *you* can see it!" He called in Trevor. "Can you see a line?"

"Oh no, it's just your imagination," said Trevor, "no one is going to notice a line." I left feeling vaguely reassured, just as I'm sure the emperor felt when those weavers told him that the clothes he was wearing were beautiful.

I spent the day looking into the mirror, turning my head side to side. I was sure I could see a line. I went back to the optical shop twice that day to get reassurances from the little tailors. "OK, once in a while, there is a line, but it's hardly noticeable," chirped Trevor.

"Oh, those glasses are just *beautiful*," chimed Mo.

Feeling sufficiently confident, I headed over to my son's school to pick him up. I had barely entered the building when one of David's first-grade classmates approached me. "You know, you have a crack in your glasses," he said as he reached up to run his grubby finger across the offending line.

I thought, "This is a fluke, a bratty kid just trying to get attention."

I continued on. Soon David's best friend, Charlie, accosted me. "Nice glasses, but did you know they have cracks in them?" He reached up to place his hands on the lenses. They just *had* to touch those cracks.

I knew by then I had been duped. Mo and Trevor were in fact telling this vain emperor what she wanted to hear. And of course the kids took it upon themselves to tell her the ugly truth.

A few years ago, when I was teaching fourth grade, I needed to get a filling replaced on a back tooth. The dentist replaced it with a beautiful gold crown. When he sat back to admire his work, he handed me a mirror. Right away, I noticed the gleam of gold. When I asked him if it perhaps showed a little too much, he assured me, "No, it's a bottom tooth, and it's way in the back. Those never show."

Once again little kids, this time my students, told me the not-so-pretty truth. "Is that tooth real gold?" was the inevitable question. After a year of kids screwing their heads around to get a look at this little gold mine in the back of my mouth, I gave up. I now have a white porcelain crown, and the comments have stopped.

I'd like to know what's wrong with these kids. Don't they know they should smile and shut up when someone enters the room wearing an ugly suit or a bad hairdo?

On the other hand, maybe they're doing us a service. Who needs a mirror when you have a kid nearby?

So gals, next time you're going out for a fancy night on the town, don't ask your spouse or significant other, "How do I look?" Ask a kid. He or she will be more than happy to tell you. You may not like what you hear, and it may cost you. You may have to get a new tooth or a new pair of glasses, but at least you'll know the truth. And you won't have to wait for a kid on the street to yell, "Look, the emperor is wearing no clothes!" as you parade around under the illusion that you're looking just fine.

HALF A MAN AND
A FULL YARD OF LEAVES

It was a perfect fall day: wonderfully cool; the kind of cool that calls for donning a light sweatshirt and gloves, maybe a baseball cap to keep the dazzling sunshine out of your eyes. And just enough breeze to get the leaves swirling gently. Although raking is not necessarily my activity of choice, I was more than happy to get outside and stuff a few garbage bags with leaves. I enlisted my seven-year-old son's help, with the enticement of a quarter for each bag filled.

David and I were actually a good little team. I raked, he loaded leaves into bags, I pressed the leaves down, and he tied the bags up. We should have left it at that. But no, David got it into his head that his friend Michael ought to be part of it. You know, many hands make light work, that sort of thing. Not to mention that he thought his buddy ought to get in on a good deal: getting paid to pick up a pile of leaves and throw them into a bag. I told him that that would be fine; after all, we would get this work done a lot faster if we had a third worker. I told David to call Michael, and be sure to have him bring a rake.

Michael reported for duty within minutes, his face beaming. The first sign that maybe this was not going to go according to plan was the absence of any type of garden tool in his hands. When I asked him about it, his response of "Huh?," accompanied by a shrug of the shoulders told me we were off to a shaky start. No matter. I handed him a rusty old rake from the garage. I figured that with just a few specific instructions to my little workers we ought to be moving like the well-oiled machine we had been; only now it would be faster.

There is an old saying, and it goes like this: "One boy is half a man, and two boys are nothing." I hadn't understood its meaning until that day. What was once a pretty efficient team effort quickly disintegrated into two knuckleheaded boys wrestling, laughing, and jumping head first into the leaves, while the mother screamed: "Get out of the pile of leaves!" "Don't throw the leaves into the air, put them in the trash bag!" "Watch out! You almost hit me in the head with the rake!" Exasperated, I told them we were done, and they dashed off to play in the tree fort. I was left raking up the scattered piles of leaves, remembering again why I do not like raking very much.

So two boys are in fact nothing, at least when it comes to getting the necessary chores done. Still, these guys just might have something to teach me. Could it be that the dreadful task of raking (and the looming task of shoveling snow) can be turned into fun? Could there be a happy medium between throwing leaves in the air, and throwing them into a garbage bag? I'll have to think about that.

As for now, Michael has gone home and I am left with half a man. Not to mention half a yard… filled with leaves, still needing to be raked. Maybe we'll try again tomorrow.

SHOP 'TIL WE DROP

Lately there's been a commercial on television for a major department store. The doors open and an attractive mother and daughter rush in. They turn in a circle, arms spread wide as if to say, "We have finally found paradise, so let's shop." I can only wonder what this must feel like.

When it comes to shopping, my daughter is nothing like these shopping enthusiasts. She thinks of shopping as a chore, one to be gotten through by planting your hands firmly in your pockets and staying within two feet of your mother at all times. I take a step, she takes a step. I say, "Isn't this nice?" She says, "Huh?" It's like pulling an elephant through a straw.

I knew we had hit rock bottom when we walked through a store last week. We were shopping *oh so slowly* for bedspreads. As we entered the store, I said, "Is there anything you need that we should be shopping for? Any clothes you need? Jackets? Shoes?" Now, can you imagine someone saying to you, "What do you need or want? *I will buy it for you.*" Your own personal sugar mama.

Her response was, of course, "No," making her the only eleven-year-old child on the entire planet willing to decline an offer that came with an open checkbook.

If you pay any attention to the television ads and newspaper circulars, we are all supposed to love shopping. Shopping is recreation.

My daughter seems to have missed this idea, and, I must admit, so have I. While her response to the dreaded shopping trip is to drag her feet, I have an opposite reaction: I am a power shopper. I shop by throwing piles of pants and sweaters over my arm, and I buy 'em all. I come home, force my children to try them on, keep one or two items and return the rest.

My husband thinks I'm crazy. He believes there's a little something wrong with shopping for your children without them being present. Like I'm their personal shopping service, and all they have to do is tear their eyes away from *America's Funniest Home Videos* long enough to give a thumbs up or down to the latest selection. He is right, of course. But believe me, we mothers try to do what causes us the least amount of pain, and you can guess which option is easier at our house.

I admit that I am a little wistful when I see the pictures of mother-daughter shopping trips (something I *never* did with my own mother by the way, once again proving the "apple doesn't fall far from the tree" theory), but I'll get over it.

There must be other ways my daughter and I can enjoy each other's company. Let's just hope we don't have to go shopping to find it.

STAYING HOME

Six years ago an immense thunderstorm tore through our neighborhood. The meteorologists called it "straight line winds," but we were never convinced. What else but a full-fledged tornado could have caused such damage? Of all the trees in our yard, only one brave birch remained standing, as if to say to the huge evergreen lying at its feet, "See, I told you, if you had just hung on a little longer, you could have made it." The evergreen groaned in response as the "tree guy" cut her up.

It just so happens that my sister-in-law, her husband Matt, and their daughter were staying with us that night. When we awoke to a very dark house, no power, and no phone service, Matt started packing his bags. He was getting out of town, and now. We couldn't understand his hurry; it wasn't as if we were going anywhere, being that my van was sitting in the driveway, crushed by a felled maple tree. But Matt's van was parked on the street and had managed to dodge the flying trees. He packed it up, put the wife and kid inside, and sped away, back to their little home in Iowa. We were baffled. What was it that compelled him to get home?

I was thinking about that a few weeks ago as I talked to my parents in Naples, Florida. You know, the city that the Weather Channel kept showing every ten minutes being battered by 125-mph winds from Hurricane Wilma? I called my dad, assuming that he and Mom were packing up *their* van to hightail it out of town, but no such luck. They weren't budging: "We have tape on the windows, water in the bathtub, and candles in the bathroom. We have a three-day supply of water and food. We're not going anywhere." This from my seventy-seven-year-old father. I was again baffled. What could it be that kept their stubborn souls tied to that house, when they could be safe and comfortable in a motel?

The answer, of course, is "home." It seems that the same feeling that motivated Matt to flee in the early morning hours to his little house next to a corn field in the middle of Iowa was the same feeling that kept my parents moored to their condo next to a golf course in Florida. And it's perhaps the same feeling that some of the survivors of Hurricane Katrina had, the ones who *could* have gotten out, yet refused. As one hanger-on in New Orleans said, "This is my house. This is my roof." And that seemed to say it all.

Those of us who are blessed to have a place to call home, be it a mansion, an apartment, or a friend's couch, understand our good fortune, and for many of us, gale-force winds are not enough to tear us away.

think it's not because of the money we have poured into our homes, for things like new roofs, nice TV sets, and a new garage, but rather because our homes are such an integral part of our family lives. My own home holds the crib where I laid my newborn daughter when I first brought her home from the hospital. Here's the banister where my son hit his head, resulting in a lot of blood and a few stitches. Here's the dining room where we say grace each night before eating. And here's the pillow where I get to lay my head at the end of each and every day.

My dad tells me he will have to repair the window screens that the hurricane destroyed in the early dawn hours, just as we had to spend hours planting trees in our decimated yard. But we are so blessed. We have a home, and it survived. And we're staying put.

THE WAITING GAME

As I sit in this dark, dusty hallway, groups of sweaty, costumed characters squeezing by me, some carrying juggling pins, others hoisting unicycles over their shoulders, I wonder, how did I get here? How at the age of forty-two, did I end up in the back of this hot, crowded circus theatre with clowns, acrobats, and daredevils pushing in to my sensible self? I am there because I am a mother.

My son, David, is nine years old. He is bright, creative, funny, sweet, and sensitive. He also has more letters attached to his name than a government agency. These letters are meant to describe and define him. *ADD* stands for attention deficit disorder, which explains why he seldom hears my directions the first, second, or sometimes even the third time. *OCD* stands for obsessive-compulsive disorder, explaining why he needs to do the same things in the same order day after excruciating day. At age three, *UPJ obstruction* meant that he would need surgery to repair a damaged kidney.

Then there are the words. *Anxiety* describes the overwhelming feelings he gets in new situations; *depression* explains why even when he was a little baby, he woke from his naps with uncontrollable tears. And just as the alphabet and all these words help define him, in an ironic quirk of fate, the alphabet is useless to him. *Dyslexia* renders letters, sounds, and the words they form unrecognizable.

What this all means to him and to me, his mother, is that a sizable chunk of his life, and therefore, my life, is spent waiting. We spend hours in waiting rooms. Waiting to see the psychiatrist, the psychologist, the speech therapist, and the reading specialist. Waiting for the next new diagnosis, the next new drug, the next new plan.

There are many times when I wonder what I would do with my time if we didn't have all these appointments. I would get a job. I would write a book. Right now I could write a sort of a travel guide on this city's best and worst waiting rooms. I can tell you that the most expensive doctors (as in psychiatrists) have the crummiest waiting rooms, filled with old greasy magazines and children's toys you don't dare allow your child to touch.

David goes in to see the doctor, and I wait some more. It can be a lonely business, unless you're lucky enough to find someone you think you might be able to talk with. I enjoy my talks with Bianca—she is as stunned as I am that her nine-year-old boy does not yet know how to read. Other days I watch. My favorite subject is the fat man with his three kids. He scoops up the little girls onto his wide lap and reads to them. He kisses his big boy's "owie." He adores his children. On days when I am feeling sorry for myself, I think of Barbara whom I met in the speech therapy waiting room, which, by the way, ranks very near to the bottom of my waiting room list, due to poor reading light and annoyingly loud siblings. Barbara told me she had been sitting in the waiting room twice a week for nine years. I thought, "I will never complain again."

But David knows none of this. He is a happy child who hops out of the car and races to his friend Michael's house as soon as we pull into the driveway, released from the latest waiting room. And he is what my friend Margaret calls "a little Bohemian boy." One who loves to draw, paint, dance, and perform.

And so, in addition to signing him up for appointments, I sign him up for circus theatre. He has just found his little piece of Nirvana: he gets to be a clown. A pratfalling, juggling, rubber-faced clown, who entertains the folks in the bleachers.

On the first day of the circus performance, I walk David backstage. And that's when I know I should have packed my novel. There are hordes of children running and hollering. What we would call mayhem. To David it's just one huge anxiety-laden stew of misbehaving children. As he clutches my hand, I know I'm not going anywhere. And so I sit, and wait, in this sweltering hall filled with performers waiting to be called onstage.

When he sees the misery on my face, he whispers, "Sorry, Mom."

I perk up, knowing he needs this reassurance. "That's OK, buddy, whatever you need to feel comfortable, that's what I'll do." And I mean it.

The next night I know to bring a book for me, a drawing pad for him, and a couple of flashlights. And even though the trapeze artists and the unicyclists keep jostling us as we sit on the dusty floor, we continue doing what we do. We'll wait together until his act comes on. And although I'm surprised to be sitting amongst the clowns and the acrobats, I am satisfied. Right now it is my job. I am his mother, and that is what a mother does. That is what this mother does.

THE MARBLE TOURNAMENT

It was the sign that caught my eye. In fact, it beckoned to me every time I passed by the little shop on St. Clair Avenue. "Marble Tournament, Saturday, August 11. Prizes… Fame and Glory…" I don't know, was it the prizes or the fame and glory? Maybe it was mere curiosity that caused me to drag my two kids to that toy shop to see what was going on. Too bad for us, the tournament had just ended. We'd made it in time for the prizes. And what prizes they were. My children stood with their mouths agape as brilliant marbles were handed out to the lucky winners. Hand-made orbs with spirals of color running through the clear glass, they looked pretty enough to eat, and certainly too beautiful to even considering knocking around on the floor. And the final prize for each participant: a large multicolored "millennium marble." My young son turned to me and asked incredulously, "Why didn't *we* play in this tournament?"

Why indeed? The thought that we could be walking off with these glorious little prizes knocking around in our pockets was just too much to take. After the crowd cleared, I asked the proprietor, the official organizer of this tournament, what it would take to be a part of this competition. He said, "Just show up next year and play." I immediately pleaded ignorance, but Mr. Fletcher wasn't letting me off the hook. He said he would show us how. Soon my children and I were on our hands and knees in a lot behind the store. A circle was drawn in the dust, and we took turns trying to knock each other's marbles out, with a deft flick of the finger. It was hot, it was dirty, but it really was fun.

It's funny what memories a game of marbles can bring back. There I was, a nine-year-old girl in her dress (girls were not allowed to wear pants to school then, even in the frigid Wisconsin winters), kneeling in the piles of dirt around our schoolyard, trying to win my opponents' marbles. I don't know how we played it; I just recall holes dotting the little hillside of our schoolyard, looking like a colony of prairie dogs had taken up residence in the neighborhood.

When we got home my daughter tied the two ends of a big string together, arranged it in a circle, and challenged me to a game.

Now, who is to say what motivates people like us to get down on all fours to hit a marble around the floor? Perhaps for me it was the nostalgic feeling I had for those games played at Franklin Elementary. Maybe too it was Mr. Fletcher's infectious spirit for the game. But I'm pretty sure that I could see the visions of those lovely little marbles in my children's eyes. And I knew how they felt. Those beautiful little globes he was giving out were just begging to be rolled around in the palm of my hand.

The three of us were promptly down on our hands and knees, tongues sticking out the side of our mouths, rear ends in the air, fingers poised. The marble tournament will return next year, and we're gonna be ready.

THE WAR OF THE WEEDS

One of my clearest childhood memories is a view of my mother's behind. Looking out my bedroom window each and every spring and summer day I would see her in her beloved garden, slumped over the perennials, bucket in one hand, trowel in the other. She was pulling weeds, which is pretty much how she spent her whole summer. I remember that she would occasionally emerge, full of dirt and sweat, long enough to change my baby sister's diaper or to get lunch for my dad. I assumed that this is what grown-up women did all summer: tended gardens, children, and husbands, in that order. And I thought I would grow to do the same thing. But while I don't usually mind tending children and husbands (in that order), I have never grown to love tending the garden.

Here's the part I do love: going to the nursery and picking out the showiest plants and bringing them home in the back of my station wagon. After a short nap, and if the weather is cooperating (that is, not too hot or too cold or too rainy or too windy), I plant the flowers in the dirt. Then I sit back and watch my garden grow. Visions of glorious blossoms fill my head as I page through the latest *People* magazine. But just as soon as that purple flower, whose name I can't remember, starts to show its lovely blossom, the party crashes. In walks big old Mrs. Dandelion on the arm of her buddy, Creeping Charlie, so named because he certainly does creep everywhere where he is not wanted. I have to put down my coffee, go out to the garden, bend down, and yank at them. And they do not want to leave. I threaten them with chemical sprays—they laugh. They'll be back, and they'll be bringing their pals. After a few days pulling and cursing at those ugly weeds, I'm ready to plow the whole thing under.

I sent an e-mail to my mother, asking, "How could you have spent all those hours weeding?" There must have been something in it for her, other than the fact that she could get away from five screaming kids, a husband, and a dog.

Here is how she responded, and I quote: "First of all, gardening is a creative outlet for me. It's true, each year there was the weed problem. But for me it was rather like making things right again—giving my precious things a chance to shine. So in that sense, it wasn't such a chore." Honestly, she puts me to shame.

My mother continued her discourse on the joys of weeding in a second message: "I just got an e-mail from a good friend and she talked about weeding her huge garden. It sounded to me like was she was tackling it like a vendetta against an enemy. So that is perhaps the way another person would view the job."

Yes, it appears that this "other person" and I have a lot in common. And when you put it that way, "a vendetta against an enemy," it certainly does not paint a very flattering picture.

So, perhaps I need an attitude adjustment. Maybe there is a way of viewing these weeds as just an impediment, not an enemy. I don't need to pull out the big guns and the chemical sprays. Just a little hand-to-hand combat, nothing too frantic or hysterical, is all that's needed.

Today I will start anew, with a new definition of weeding. Pulling weeds is not a war; it is simply a way to let my precious flowers grow. A few tugs at Creeping Charlie, and a couple whacks at yet another dandelion, and soon I'll be done. I'll pour myself a cup of coffee, settle back, and watch those flowers grow. My mother will be proud.

THE PERFECT MOM

As I pack my ten-year-old son's lunch with homemade vegan granola, satsuma oranges from Oregon, organic vanilla yogurt, and free-range chicken breast tenders, I feel a deep sense of satisfaction. I know that I am providing the best meal possible for my little one. I am a perfect mom... But then I throw in a bag of cheese puffs and cream-filled cupcakes. I am, in fact, a perfect fraud.

It all has to do with the perfect mom next door. Everyone has a mom like this in her neighborhood—the kind of parent who finds just the right food, the perfect venue for a birthday party, and an educational summer vacation. My perfect mom just happens to be the mother of my son's best friend. So I get daily exposure to her faultless ways. My fellow fraud parent, Nancy, calls it "enrichment parenting." Nancy and I, on the other hand, throw a PB&J sandwich in our kids' lunches, sign them up for swimming lessons at the crummy city pool, and make plans to spend our summer vacations at the waterpark in Wisconsin Dells. We love our kids every bit as much as the perfect parent; it's just that we aren't so pretty about it. In fact, we are downright messy as we pick up our kids in the van with the cookie crumbs all over the seat. I throw my son a pair of sweatpants and tell him to put them on in the car: we're late for karate. Meanwhile the perfect mom pulls up in her clean SUV, as she prepares to drive her son to advanced Spanish classes.

There are exactly three things that are infuriating about these types of moms. First, one cannot help but feel oh-so-inferior around these gals. Even if I stay up all night making a Tin Man costume for my son (which would never ever happen, but let's just hypothesize here), the perfect mom would have stayed up even longer and made a witch costume, complete with flying monkeys that she had imported from the Amazon.

Second, one cannot become one of these moms just by trying, no matter how hard. It seems to be to be bred into their genes. I try, I really do, to be perfect, but then something happens like the dog throws up on the carpet right before the birthday party, or my daughter throws a tantrum. Something always makes me come up short.

But here's the last part of this perfection that's really annoying: these moms are not wholly unlikable. I wish I could hate this mother, if only because I feel like a bumbling idiot when I'm around her. But I can't. Because she has developed the ability to be nice, really nice. She smiles when she tells me that her older child scored a perfect score on the ACT. In fact, she doesn't even seem to comprehend the fact that she is perfection itself and I am but a groveling idiot. (Or maybe she secretly revels in her superiority at night.)

In any case, there is no use tampering with perfection. We cannot change the perfect mom, and heaven knows we imperfect moms are beyond repair. So, we're inferior, and we might as well accept it, because there's only room at the top for one. I'm down here at the bottom with my fellow fraudsters. We do our best, though, and celebrate when we get near her level. And because she is so darn nice, we let her have her place on top.

THE GUEST WHO
WOULDN'T GO AWAY

There's a man in my husband's office who was fired a few months ago. That is, everyone *thinks* he was fired. Word is that Roger was "encouraged to look elsewhere" for a position. But here's the kicker: the guy refuses to go away. Every day Roger shows up grinning, tucks himself into his cube, and gets down to work. He tags along when the gang goes out to lunch. He even had the audacity to attend the office Christmas party! Joking, smiling, shaking hands, as if he had every reason to be there! The office buzz is that he even talks to people about work in the *future* tense, statements like "When we put out the marketing plan in May..." or "When we host the salespeople from Japan..." Get the picture? He's not going anywhere!

This smiley little rascal has been talked to more than once. Lots of suggestions, even some pretty firm nudges. By God, they have even talked about giving his cube up to someone else when the office goes through reorganization next month. His name's not on the cube map, but what does that matter? Undaunted, this guy drives up in his little car every day, parks, gets his cup of coffee, and just keeps on a-workin' as if he has every right to be there, for Pete's sake.

All this puts me in mind of unwelcome guests in general, people who just won't go away, even when all signals suggest that it's time to move on.

Recently, my husband, children, and I were visiting my parents over a long weekend. We had planned on staying three nights. But on the last night, we figured, what the heck, the kids are having so much fun, why not stay another night? We did. Wouldn't you know, the next day was even more fun than the one before. I said to my mom, "I know we said we'd leave at ten. Maybe we'll wait until after lunch." My sweet mother looked at me and said, "That's fine." Then, with a pause and a slightly pained expression, she added, "Just so you leave before dinner." I must admit I was a little bit shocked. Could it be we were becoming those unwelcome guests you hear about? The ones that hang on just a little too long, until their smiling greeting in the morning gets to feel like nails on a chalkboard?

I wonder if we're all a little like Roger, moving blissfully along, unaware that the welcome mat was rolled up long ago.

Some might say it's the responsibility of the guest to figure out when it's time to move on. I say, let's leave it to the host. Let them do the kicking out, because face it, we're all convinced that no one ever wants us to leave.

Someone needs to invent a universal phrase or sign that will communicate, "Hey, your time is up." Like the not-so-subtle signal my husband gives me at a party that lets me know I have a bit of spinach between my teeth. Just a notification that will let us exit gracefully.

In the meantime, I really hope Roger gets the message, and soon. He can stash the welcome mat in the back of his car before he drives away. And we can all breathe a sigh of relief.

FEELING BLUE

The choice was easy. After years of staring at the lackluster beige-and-white marbled wallpaper throughout my house, it was time for a change. After peeling away that ugly paper, I finally got to pick the color I've always wanted… blue.

I quickly packed up my purse and drove to the paint store. I rifled through the swatches, but it didn't take long. There it was, and it was called "Northern Air." A rich shade, reminiscent of a clear summer morning sky.

That evening I showed my husband the swatch. "Blue?" After a long pause, he added, "I just didn't think that would be the color. Won't that be too dark? Won't that be too, well… blue?" As a compromise, he suggested we pick a lighter shade of blue. Not sky blue, more like baby blue, as in "Silvery Blue." I told him I would think about it. My sister came over to register her opinion. I was excited to show her the choices of blue, knowing full well she would choose my "Northern Air" over some boring light blue.

Her first reaction? "Blue? Blue? I'm just so surprised! I was thinking, I don't know, beige or off-white. But blue? That's just so… blue!" My confidence was slipping.

I called my friend Rita, the interior designer. You can guess her reaction. She helped me pick out some nice subdued shades of beige. Seeing my disappointment she said, "OK, if you really want blue, how about a lighter shade, say 'Under the Big Top'?"

In the background, witnessing this excruciating process were Richie and Dave, the painters. They stayed busy painting the trim "Dove White," while I mulled over the possibilities of beiges. After all the advice-givers made their exits, they came to me, paintbrushes and rollers in hand. They told me that they in fact *liked* the blue. "Sorry," I told them. "We clearly do not know what we are doing. 'Northern Air' is just not right." So they did as I told them: tried out different samples of beige and light blue on my walls so we could see how they looked. The three of us stood back, gazing at the various shades. Beige was, well, beige. A variation on what I had been staring at for years. The light blue looked like a baby's nursery. It had come down to this: beige, light beige, or light blue. Maybe even white. I was sad. Deflated. My walls no longer presented themselves as an opportunity for expression and joy. Instead, I had let them become a place for everyone else to register his or her opinion.

Finally, in his low gravelly tone, Dave said, "You know, me and Richie have been talking. It seems you just don't trust your own instincts. Because you know what you like. You've known it all along. Now, why don't you let me go pick up a gallon of 'Northern Air'?"

No longer knowing what to do, I acquiesced. I flopped on the couch, waved my hand, and said, "Go ahead, might as well try it." He and Richie returned from the paint store and painted great swaths of brilliant blue onto my walls. We laughed. We congratulated each other. I nearly cried. It was beautiful. My walls look like a clear summer morning sky.

These walls now give me pure delight. I smile at the blue. I revel in the blue. And I knew I would, all along.

THE FALL DOG

It's about the last thing you want to see when you walk into your house: a large dark stain on the carpet. A few weeks ago, it was an ugly scratch on the dining room table. Before that, a crack in the window. Just another of the many little household mishaps and messes that seem to happen every day. And, as with all things that annoy us, we have to have someone to blame. I used to yell at the kids for the disarray and disrepair in the house. Now I've found a new scapegoat. His name is Chester. And he is only too happy to take the blame— just as long as you keep feeding him and taking him on walks around the block.

Our poor dog. A few years ago we brought this lovable little guy into our lives. Thinking he was being adopted into a loving home, he probably thanked his little puppy stars. Little did he know that he would become the whipping boy, the punching bag, the blame receptacle for every little problem in this house. A tear in the upholstery? Must have been the dog. Scratches in the woodwork? It was the pooch. A spot in the carpet? We all know where that came from.

I wonder what other families, the ones without dogs, do to explain their house's messy mistakes. At our house, the blame used to start at the bottom of the rung, namely the children. No wonder my kids were so happy to get this dog. Now, instead of getting hollered at for muddy prints on the carpet, they can just look to Chester, and before he even has a chance to howl in protest, he's in a laundry tub getting his paws scrubbed.

It's even worse with repair people. They really want to know who the culprit was. Whenever I call someone to my house to fix some damage, the first thing their eyes light on is the pooch. "Oh, you have a dog," they say with a sigh, as if that explains the leaky faucet. It's gotten to the point that when a service truck pulls in, Chester retreats to his kennel, tail tucked and ears flat. He knows he's in trouble again, he just doesn't know why.

Recently I called a service technician to clean that stain on the carpet. The carpet guy took one look at Chester, and declared, "It was the dog, wasn't it?" I had to admit that, in fact, Chester had vomited a few weeks ago and—not to be too graphic here—the only thing that landed on the carpet was a small puddle of bright yellow bile. OK, so this time it really was the dog's fault. But the carpet guy kept referring to the offending fluid as "vile," not bile, but "vile" as in, "Well, I don't know if my carpet stain remover works on *dog vile*." I thought I must have heard him wrong, but no, he kept talking about the "dog vile," and how he just didn't see how anything could remove "dog vile." He even wrote it on the invoice. Perhaps this all reflected his attitude toward dogs and the stains they leave behind. Vile, indeed.

I know that this blame game could never work for cat owners. No, cat owners have no one but themselves (and their children) to blame for household messes. Imagine trying to pin the blame on a cat. A haughty flick of a tail combined with a look of indignation, as if to say, "Are you kidding? Me? Scratches on the leather couch? I don't think so," would put an end to any accusations.

Household damage is bound to occur, and we all need someone to blame. Maybe the dog is taking a bit more of the heat than he deserves. After all, he is just a seventeen-pound miniature poodle who lies around, minding his own business. But he doesn't seem to care, and it all seems to work out just fine. I get someone to holler at, my children get someone else to take the fall, and Chester gets his nightly meal. The windows keep breaking, the furniture is falling apart, and the carpet is always dirty, but somehow everyone is happy.

A DECISIVE DECORATOR

My husband and I are a pathetically indecisive team, especially when it comes to decorating our house. Samples of paint colors cover our hallway walls; torn pieces of wallpaper are taped to the kitchen cupboards. Which one to choose?

First, there was the living room carpet decision. We spent weeks visiting carpet stores, listening to lectures on the value of a tighter weave, the advantages of nylon over wool (or was it the other way around?), and promise after promise that "this carpet absolutely will not stain." We were overwhelmed. Finally, out of sheer exhaustion, we picked one. Actually, I think I picked it. My husband had long since moved on to another drawn-out decorating decision. For two years we have had this carpet, and for two years we have not liked it. It's just not right. Our indecision has quickly turned into buyer's remorse.

Then came the quest to find a leather couch for our family room. We picked one; we bought it. And it too just wasn't right. Too short. Too stiff. We returned it. My thirteen-year-old daughter, Christine, remarked, "You know, you should have just gotten that big brown soft leather couch I pointed out at that first store we went to. It was comfortable, we could stretch out, and it was cheap." My husband and I looked at each other… she was right. But we hadn't listened to her. It was my first inkling that maybe this child had a better eye for decoration (and a better ability to make a decision) than her wishy-washy parents did. Maybe we should have taken her along when we picked out the carpet.

A few months later, I decided we needed some new carpeting for the basement. Having learned a lesson from the first carpet debacle, I brought home what I thought were some suitable samples from the store. Christine shook her head. "No, Mom, those are way too dark." The next time, I was smart enough to take her to the carpet store. She walked in the door, walked over to a roll of carpet leaning up against the wall, and said, "Get this." I wondered if she was right, but I knew not to question her. We got it. It is a lovely golden plush. No remorse there. We love it.

So, it happens that I have a little decorator at my house. We (mom, dad, and brother) are singing her praises: a natural designer has been born to our family. Christine, however, sees it as no big deal. She simply thinks of it as having the ability to make a decision, with no looking back. She gets home in time to watch *CSI: Miami,* and I have a beautiful basement rug.

Last week I took her to the carpet store again, this time to pick out a rug for our bedroom. Christine wasn't feeling well, but I really wanted to pick out a rug that very day, so she acquiesced. Thank goodness they had a little table and chairs so she could rest her head while the salesperson brought out the samples. I hemmed and hawed. Christine lifted her head, pointed to a sample, and said, "Get that one." All done with a lift of the head and ten minutes to spare on the parking meter. And it's just right.

So now I'm saving up my money. I'm hoping that I'll have enough so I can replace this dreadful living room carpet before Christine goes off to college. I'm sure she'll pick out the exact right thing, in only fifteen minutes, and we'll love it.

LESSONS FROM A LITTLE BABY

Last week my thirteen-year-old daughter came home with a baby. Christine called me on the phone, "Mom, you have to come pick me up! No way am I carrying this baby on the school bus." I did as instructed, pulling into the junior high parking lot to look for my girl, now a young woman (she did have a baby, didn't she?). Out she strutted, furtively glancing side to side to see if anyone could be noticing that she was carrying a bundle of baby wrapped up in a fuzzy pink blanket. She plopped down into the seat. "Thank goodness she didn't cry," she said as she shoved the infant into my arms. "Here, Mom, you hold her, I have to check my braces in the mirror. And whatever you do, don't let her head fall back; she'll start crying."

Perhaps I should explain. This was not a real baby, although you wouldn't know it by the lifelike sounds coming from its battery-powered sound box. This was a simulated baby, sent home for the weekend by the home economics teacher, for the purpose of teaching young adolescents the perils of young pregnancy and parenthood. It was the same size and weight as a real baby, although a great deal harder to the touch, and as I mentioned, it made the same sounds. Especially when I let her head fall back as I adjusted my seat belt.

Suddenly a cry emanated not so much from its mouth as from its stomach. But it was real all right. "I told you, Mom, not to let its head fall!" The exasperated teen instructing the inexperienced mom who had never heard a baby cry before.

The baby would not stop crying, despite my best rocking. I handed the baby back to my daughter (we still had not gotten out of the parking lot). "Here, try feeding her or rocking her, or changing her diaper. I'm driving."

The baby, who had been christened "Little Baby Coco" by the girl who had kept her the weekend before, cried the whole way home. Finally, after fifteen minutes of constant rocking, feeding, and diaper changing, Coco stopped crying. This little experiment was getting pretty close to reality. Babies do indeed cry. They often cry for no apparent reason, and then miraculously, they stop—again, for no apparent reason.

Soon, it was time for supper. Coco started to cry. Now, this was getting a little *too* realistic for me. It wasn't until my children reached age three that we could all sit down together for dinner without a child crying, whining, having a tantrum, or getting sick. I told Christine that she would need to leave the table so that she could comfort the baby while we ate. As soon as she returned, Coco commenced to wail. Christine's brother pleaded, "Make it stop!" We all agreed. Dad took the baby (careful not to let its head drop) and started to carry it to the garage. Desperate times call for desperate measures.

"You can't do that!" my daughter yelled. "I'll get a bad grade!" Not to mention the fact that this was *not* what we want to be teaching our daughter about caring for an infant.

Finally, and only because my daughter was at this point starving, her brother was pulling on his hair, the dog was hiding, and her parents were fighting, Christine agreed to let the baby be put in the bathroom. "But only with the door closed, so the dog doesn't chew on her!" My husband piled blankets on the wailing offender and closed the door. Then we ate dinner in silence. Now here's a sickeningly familiar feeling: taking a bite, and waiting and listening. "Hey, I think she stopped crying!"… No, she was just taking a deep breath to power her next wail. And so it went, eating, stopping, listening, sighing.

We rescued Little Baby Coco from the bathroom, and I got out the instruction manual, the one we all wish our babies had come with. It said, "Baby can be turned off by putting the end of a paper clip in the tiny hole in its back." I went for the paper clip. My daughter protested, "But I'll get a bad grade!" Within two minutes the baby was crying, and Christine grabbed the paper clip out of my hand, and shoved it into the tiny hole. Soon there was silence.

My daughter returned Little Baby Coco the next day, along with a written plea from her mother that she not receive a bad grade.

And what did my daughter learn from this? Well, perhaps to be abstinent. Forever. Or perhaps she learned that babies (and children) cry... and whine, and just plain drive you crazy. And sometimes you do want to put them in the garage for a while, just a little while. But you don't do that. Sometimes you have to lock yourself (not the baby) in the bathroom while you calm down.

I hope she doesn't think babies come with instruction manuals, and I certainly hope she doesn't think there is some kind of "off" button on the baby for those times when a parent can't take it anymore.

But there was one lesson Coco could not teach my daughter, a lesson I am reminded of every time I see my kids walk in the door at the end of the day. No matter how big the annoyance, whether it be crying or bad grades, or threatening to run away from home, I have never wished *not* to be a mother to these children. It really is worth the tears, the frustration, and the sleepless nights. No plastic baby could ever simulate that feeling. My daughter will have to find that out on her own. Someday.

THIS NEVER-ENDING GAME

I thought I was done decorating. After twelve years in this old house, nearly every wall had been painted, every floor covered with new carpet or tile. Wood floors refinished. New drapes, new furniture, new windows installed. I was fairly satisfied. No, really satisfied. But just as I sat down to admire the fruits of my efforts, my fourteen-year-old daughter had to spoil the whole celebration: "Mom, you know, the kitchen could really do with a more modern look."

I raised my weary head from the couch. What could she possibly be talking about? The cupboards were old and original, that's true, but the heavy oak doors with the brass handles looked just fine. The strawberry and vine wallpaper was cheery, still relatively clean and decorative. The white Formica counters were very functional, perhaps scratched and a little gouged by knives over the years, but still quite adequate. So, what wasn't to like?

Christine pointed out, "Just take a look at the family room. Everything in here is modern, with blacks and beiges and greens. The cabinet doors are a light wood finish with silver handles. The floors are tile, the rug a perfect shade of green. You did a great job. But then you look over at the kitchen, and frankly, Mom, it seems pretty darned old-fashioned. Like it came from your childhood, or something. Time for a new look." With this withering appraisal, she grabbed a granola bar and traipsed upstairs to do her homework. My little decorator had spoken.

And so it had begun, what I call the domino effect of home decorating. Every homeowner experiences it: fix up the living room and soon the sunroom right next to it begs for a makeover. Install new cabinets in the den, and the dining room is whining for its own cabinets. It's only fair, after all. Spruce up the downstairs bathroom with new fixtures, suddenly the upstairs bathroom is complaining about its old leaky sink. On and on it goes. Like painting the Golden Gate Bridge: you get to the last section, you're ready to pour yourself a cup of coffee and enjoy the view, when all of a sudden the paint starts peeling on the first section of the bridge. So you get up and start painting all over again.

Well, I argued to myself, at least the kitchen's counters were fine. Who can argue with white countertops? My mother-in-law, that's who. When I told her about my daughter's assessment of the kitchen, I expected her complete support. Something like, "Oh, this kitchen is lovely. I wouldn't change a thing." Instead she stomped all over it.

She did in fact say, "You know, I think this kitchen is just fine." I breathed a sigh of relief and nodded smugly. (See, Christine? I told you.) But oh, she had to keep talking: "The one thing I would change though, dear, is these counters. If you got new counters, this kitchen would look so much more updated." Even my beloved counters weren't safe from my mother-in-law's quick judgment.

And so it happened that this kitchen, which was just fine a month ago, has become a real eyesore. I walk in here now and shudder at the eighties-style oak and brass cupboards. The ivy wallpaper threatens to take over my every thought; the counters are not even worthy to hold my old coffee pot. I can hardly stand to cook.

Soon I am surfing the web. I should be writing. I should be ironing. I should be volunteering at the local shelter. Instead I am secretly seeking. Looking for glossy smooth cupboard doors with polished nickel handles. Admiring shiny cobalt-blue countertops, guaranteed to resist all scratches. Sleek stainless steel appliances. Every once in a while I sneak a peek at my bank account, which shouts "No!" and slaps my hand when I inquire of its balance. We all know there's not enough in there.

After a few months of savings, I'll probably have enough to at least get new cupboard doors. Then I'll save up to get these very decent countertops replaced. I'll talk my husband into helping me remove the wallpaper, and we'll paint. And it will be lovely.

And just as I sit down to admire our latest handiwork, a kid will walk in. She'll make a throw-away comment about the dining room table or the family room furniture. Anything, just to keep this game of dominoes going on forever.

And I'll sigh, take a quick sip of coffee, pick up my can of paint, and start painting the bridge all over again.

'

A WORD OF THANKS TO
THE QUEEN MUM

It happened again. September was coming to an end, summer had passed me by, and there I was with no flower garden. Every spring I tell myself, "Move it, sister. Get out your shovel! Get out your gloves! Now, dig!," and every year I sigh and retreat to my coffee and newspaper. It's not the act of digging that has me shuddering; it's not knowing what exactly to put in the dirt that has me overwhelmed. I take walks around the neighborhood for inspiration. Inspiration turns to defeat. I ask myself, "How did they know to plant those two things together?" "Is that an annual or a perennial?" "Oh, gee, someone is throwing in handfuls of bone meal. Should I be buying that?" That's when King Procrastination steps in, telling me I've got to beware. This is way too big a task for someone so little as me, and I readily agree. Time to pour myself another cup of coffee and think about tackling that flower bed next year. Next thing you know, I'm home again, sprinkling grass seed over the dirt.

My husband was amazed and then irritated as he once again witnessed my internal battle with the garden.

"Just do it!" he admonished. "Just stick something in the ground and see if it grows!" He was right, of course. Time to take the trowel by the handle, so to speak, and get something planted.

So the next day, I woke early and drove to the nursery. I had heard that you could plant perennials in the fall. All I had to do was walk in and buy some plants. I grabbed a cart and start walking. To my amazement, there was hardly a plant in sight. In fact, most of the nursery seemed packed up and ready to go to sleep for the winter. I asked for help, and a worker named Katie was summoned. Was she suppressing a grin when I told her I was "ready to plant"? She gently took me by the arm, and informed me that yes, many types of perennials can be planted in the fall, but, unfortunately, in order for them to survive the winter, they need to be planted by the first week of September, at the very latest. I was just a few weeks too late. This seemed to be the story of my gardening life. But she did have one consolation prize for the procrastinator. And what a prize it was. The mums. These fine-looking blooms were nothing less than spectacular. Katie told me I could plant one in a large pot, and as long as I kept it from freezing, it would last well into fall.

I bought the showiest one I could find: big and yellow and full of blossoms. I lugged this showpiece home, put some dirt in a pot, and introduced the Queen Mum to her new place. There she sits on my front step. I walk outside and pretend to be a passerby. Someone, who, like me, is trying to get ideas for her garden. "My, look at that!" I tell myself, "That woman sure knows how to garden. Look at that big beautiful mum on her front step!" I just know people are admiring this miracle of nature. *And* I know that people are now making assumptions about me. They are saying, "Wow, with a flower like that in the front, just imagine what her garden looks like in the back." Never mind that it is nothing more than a bed of grass and weeds. People make assumptions, and I wouldn't want to discourage them, would I?

I am aware that this mum is a cheap date. All I have to do is plant her in a pot, put her on the step, and I become the talk of the neighborhood. But I do show my appreciation to her. During those nights of frost, I ask my husband to lug her in; I yell at the dog when he starts sniffing her, I keep the children's hands from picking her blossoms. She allows me to be the gardener I always hoped I would be, and I allow her to thrive in her little bucket.

I know that it is inevitable; this grand little lady will die after the first night I forget to haul her indoors. I will be saddened that my little show-off will be gone. But she will have left a legacy. And next time, I'll be ready… in the spring.

INDEPENDENCE DAY

Here it is, the Fourth of July, and like all good, fun-loving American citizens, my family and I are celebrating. With fireworks, picnics, and parades, we Americans rejoice in the fact that many years ago, our little bunch of colonies actually became independent from England. That nasty King George III taxed us unfairly, and essentially treated us like little children. But we broke that bond and got to be our own country, the United States of America.

Although I celebrate, I have to admit that lately I've been feeling that old King George got a bad rap. I mean, I'm starting to empathize with the guy. There he is, ruling over his "children" and then one morning, before he even has time to put on his robe and adjust his crown, he hears that these kids want to be independent. So, does he just raise his scepter and say good-bye? I should say not; he puts up a heck of a fight. A war, even; a war which of course he eventually loses. We celebrate, and he walks away sad, very sad indeed.

I too am hearing the sounds of independence rumbling through my house, and I too am ready to put up a fight. As I take a comb to my ten-year-old son's unruly hair, he pulls away, saying, "Don't comb my hair, I like it this way!" When I ask my fourteen-year-old daughter about her day, she says, "It was fine." When I press for more, she sighs, and says, "Mom, I don't need to tell you everything about my day. Really, it was fine!" What happened to the little girl who came skipping home from grade school telling me all the things that Sarah said, and all the ways that Ethan was naughty?

Yes, my children are declaring independence, and like good (or bad) King George, I am fighting it. I want them to want me. My job has been turned on its ear. Am I really just supposed to sip coffee and read the paper while my son gets himself ready for school, unassisted by me? Am I really supposed to trust that my daughter's day was fine, without my wise intervention?

Everyone tells me that this is the way it should be, that our job as parents is to teach children to depend on us less and less. Adults, by definition, should not need their parents to solve their daily problems or help them comb their hair. So, if my children are saying (and they have been saying this since they were two years old), "I can do it myself!," it's a very good thing.

I try to put a positive spin on all this independent behavior by looking at the past. I remember when my daughter no longer needed me to push her on the swing. I was free to sit on the bench and read a book. That was a good thing. I remember when I did not have to lug a diaper bag to every darned outing. My son could actually use the bathroom. That was a very good thing.

Yes, every step toward independence that I look back on, whether it was my daughter finally learning to ride a bike without me holding on, or my son actually sitting down and doing homework without my constant assistance, has been very pleasant. I've had more time to do what I want to do, like reading, or even picking up my knitting needles again. It's been good for all of us. Maybe I should look forward and trust that their continuing journey toward complete independence (also known as adulthood) can be just as good.

I hope my kids don't have to start a war with me. Because they will become independent, whether it is a pleasant process or a battle. And someday, just as we as a nation celebrate Independence Day, I too will celebrate my children's.

APPRECIATING WHAT I'VE GOT

When I left college, I came away with two things: a degree and enough houseplants to fill my parents' station wagon. Houseplants were, and perhaps continue to be, the favored method of decoration in those tiny dorm rooms. Big hardy plants that ask for nothing more than a little water and a place to spread out. They seemed to grow extra body parts overnight, like the "spider plant" that spewed forth baby arachnids as I slumbered, and the Philodendron that spread its waxy leaves across my dresser.

I moved from dorm to apartment to house, and always these little creeping creatures followed me. I can't say that I had much affection for them. They were kind of like the beer mugs and the popcorn popper I carted from place to place. They were just part of the furniture, and like the furniture, they went where I went.

Over time, I was not sorry to see these little reminders of my past fade away. When the English ivy drooped and the Ficus started dropping leaves, it was not difficult to say good-bye. Like throwing out my old beanbag chair, I felt no remorse.

I did hang on to one plant. An African violet. This little guy just kept blooming, despite the fact that it had been chewed on by the puppy, knocked over countless times by a kid or two, and left panting for water more times than I care to admit. Yes, this plant and I had come to a friendly understanding: it got to stay, as long as it understood that it might need to withstand the occasional abuse that comes with living with two kids and a dog, and that it was not to expect more than the occasional watering. This little plant with the velvet leaves and dark purple flowers was happy to cooperate, letting me know when it needed water by a doing a pathetic droop. Gosh, I was proud of that plant.

Then one day it died. Just like that. This was the first time I felt like a real "plant" person. I was sad. I had grown attached to this fuzzy bloomer, and I had thought that it would always be around. Indeed, I didn't know what I had 'til it was gone.

There is a bit of good news in all this: houseplants are easy to replace. Whereas it takes a period of grieving before one can move on from the death of the family dog, there is no such period for African violets. I went to the nearest florist, picked out a plant with the same dark purple flowers, and placed it gently into the pot.

My new plant is doing well, with one exception: since arriving at our house six months ago, it has not offered any blossoms. It's as if this plant is holding back, making sure I am worthy.

I will prove my worthiness. I will water, I will feed, and I will protect it from evil children and dogs. I have learned that plants, like people and animals, deserve our best attention, and if we love them, as I loved this little violet, they should never be taken for granted. Especially those plants who ask for nothing more than a little water and a place to grow.

SUPPER WITH OLD FRIENDS

I had supper last night with some old friends. Actually, I was the old one; they were the friends. I am now old enough to be dining with my former fourth-grade students. We didn't drink (since they are not of legal drinking age), but we did order from adult menus, and they called me by my first name. And I didn't even think to tell them to sit down, to raise their hands, or to hand in their papers.

This meeting came about after I happened to see one of these students, Leah, at the pool this summer. Over the years we had kept up sporadically, a Christmas card here, a letter there. We got to talking and she wondered if I might like to join her and Luke, another former student, for dinner. Well, why not? Old students, talking over old times with their favorite elementary school teacher.

As I walked up to the restaurant that night, I could see Luke. I couldn't see his face, but there was no mistaking the boy, now the man, in silhouette against the evening sun. The same posture, same stance, the same restless hands. When I approached him he smiled, said "Hi," and gave me a hug, a stiff embrace really.

After all, how do you hug your teacher? I wanted to press my cheek next to his for just one second, to feel that little boy inside. But of course I didn't. I asked if he had put our name in (always the one to set the rules here), and he hadn't. I was thankful for that because it gave me some time to compose myself while he went to talk to the host. I needed to walk away and clear that catch in my throat, the ache that said the little boy was gone, and in his place was an awkward, yet beautiful, nineteen-year-old man. After some self-conscious, somewhat stilted conversation, Leah arrived, looking beautiful, and oh-so-adult. We were seated at our table, and conversation flowed fairly easily, with a few pauses and bumps in the road.

These children amazed me. Luke was putting himself through college. Leah had considered studying abroad, but didn't know if she could leave her recently divorced mom and little sister for that amount of time. Luke was advising his mom to quit her job—she hated it, and he was encouraging her to move on. Leah didn't want to see her dad, she was so angry with him, but she knew that she might be making a really big mistake down the road if she didn't see him. I listened. And silently marveled. How did this happen? How did they get to the point of adulthood where they were not only responsible for themselves, but for the people around them?

Then Luke looked at me and said, "You know, I'm still awful at math. I got a C in college algebra." Again

I wanted to embrace this young man and weep. Tell him it didn't matter that he was bad at math; it *never* mattered. What mattered was the fine person he always was, and the fine person he turned out to be. I wanted to tell him that that little boy I loved in fourth grade was still there, and that math never determined the character of a person. But of course I didn't. So now I write it.

Next week my son and I will argue about him having one more peanut butter and honey sandwich for supper, a fight that exhausts and angers me. My daughter will bring home her math paper for me to explain, and again she won't understand, because she is not good at math. But now I will look at my son and know that he will turn out to be a fine young man (even if he is raised only on peanut butter and honey sandwiches) and I will look at my daughter and know she will turn out to be the wonderful person she already is. Because math doesn't matter. It's really the person inside that matters. The person I wanted to feel when I hugged Luke. Quite a dinner, and quite a lesson for an old person such as me.

MOM'S PERFECT MEAL

My daughter Christine loves to eat dinner at Grandma's house. She knows that Grandma will always be serving up her all-time favorite: oven-fried chicken. Nothing fancy, just chicken, as only my mother can make it. And that is the point. Only my mother can make it. I've asked her for the recipe; it's pretty simple. Dip the chicken pieces in milk; roll the pieces in a mixture of cornflake crumbs and seasoning salt. Bake it. I've tried, numerous times. And the response seldom varies: "Thanks, Mom, it's good," Christine says, while she pushes the pieces around the plate with her fork. Her actions speak louder than her words. It's just not right. What am I missing? Not enough seasoning salt? Maybe I need to bake it a little longer. I have to agree with her, it's OK, but just not what makes our mouths water at Grandma's house. I try hard to get it right, and my daughter tries hard to hide her disappointment. I stop trying to replicate the recipe.

The same happens with my husband's grandma's molasses cookie recipe. I have the recipe, written out in her hand on a dusty index card stained with molasses and butter. I follow it exactly. The response is predictable:

"Hmmm, these are pretty good," my husband says as he takes a bite. Yes, *pretty good.* Just not what he had wished for. Not like Grandma used to make. And so I put the recipe away. With Grandma gone, it seems that her cookies are also gone, forever.

I am baffled: just what is it that I'm missing?

I believe I got my answer last year, during the holidays. My parents, along with most of their generation, have migrated to Florida during this chilly season, and they asked us to fly down and join them for Thanksgiving. We were only too willing to oblige and escape our nasty weather. Now, my mother has been serving me turkey dinners for forty-odd years. The menu seldom varies, which is of course what we all count on at Thanksgiving and Christmas. Still, when she came out wearing shorts and a brightly flowered T-shirt, carrying the turkey on a platter... well, it felt like a charade. The turkey was there all right, along with all the fixings. But it just didn't taste the same. It seems a turkey dinner served in eighty-degree weather will never be quite right.

So there it is: the food we enjoy is more than ingredients, and more than the hours we spend trying to get it just right. I can continue to try replicate these recipes, and I will always fail. The recipe for a perfect dish? Here it is: the original cook, Mom, must prepare the recipe; the cook (again, Mom), needs to be present during the eating; the usual family members must be gathered; and the setting must not vary. The right climate, the right house, the right people... the right cook.

This year we've persuaded Grandma and Grandpa to make the trip back to Minnesota for the holidays. Sure, we are forcing them indoors in this frigid climate, when they could be out on the lanai enjoying a lemonade. But I'm selfish. I want my turkey dinner. Yes, I want the turkey, the fixings, the cold weather, and my mom serving up the food, wearing long pants and a sweater.

In the meantime, I am working on developing my own recipes—a few things that my children will love and no one will ever be able to repeat, no matter how hard they try.

A SUCCESS BEYOND MEASURE

"Face it, Mom… I'm just not good at anything." I cringed when I heard this pronouncement from my beautiful, bright fifteen-year-old daughter. These words were spoken by a girl who, like all children, had faced her young world with optimism. She could draw, she could run, she could sing. And no one, certainly not her family, nor her babysitters, her early teachers, not even her friends, told her differently. She was special, unique, and oh-so-talented.

Then something happened on that treacherous trip to adulthood. My child and her peers learned that it is not enough to believe you are good. Instead, you have to prove it. And if you cannot prove it, if you cannot stand out in a crowd with a trophy in one hand and a list of accomplishments in the other, well, you are simply not good at anything.

Christine tried out for the spring play and didn't get in. She was surprised; she thought that she was good at acting. She tried out for the school honors choir, and to her dismay, she was not a good enough singer. When I suggested that she try out for the softball team, she looked at me with that "Are you kidding?" tilt of the head, and I knew she was right. I'm afraid the girl doesn't stand a chance when it comes to sports—the genes my klutzy husband and my uncoordinated self have passed on make athletics only a dream for my daughter.

It's true: Christine is not exceptionally good at "anything." Anything being singing, acting, art, or that most important of all American pastimes, sports. In a culture that measures success by grade point average, SAT scores, and runs batted in, my daughter is a failure. How to tell her that by all other standards, the ones that matter, she is a success?

I could tell her (in fact I have told her) about my twenty-year high school reunion. By all outside measures, I was no stellar success in high school either. No sports, no honors, just fairly decent grades and good friends. Then I could tell her about Cindy Ramsey. Cindy had it all. Gorgeous, with beautiful long blonde curls. She was a cheerleader, an athlete, homecoming queen, head of the National Honor Society, and on top of that, she always had a boyfriend. I could only admire her from afar. I hate to admit it, but I was sort of hoping that when Cindy and I met up twenty years later, she would have gained fifty pounds and been looking for meaningful employment. The truth was, Cindy was doing fine. But she was doing no more fine than I was. (I even looked as good as her, and although that shouldn't matter, let's face it, it does.) I say this without bitterness or rancor toward those prom queens of my adolescence. The lesson is simply that we all even out over time.

Or I could tell my daughter, as I often do, what she is good at. She is a wonderful, clever writer and teller of stories. She has a sparkling smile and a sense of humor to go with it. She is kind as can be to her little brother, which isn't always easy, even for me. She asks me how I'm feeling, she worries about her grandma, she loves to "hang out" with her dad. Is it too cliché to say that she is good on the inside, and that's where it really counts? In fact, that that's where success really lies?

Finally, I could tell her that this question, "Am I good enough?" could possibly dog her for the rest of her days. Who among us has not wondered if we measure up to some attainable standard at home, at the office, or compared to other mothers? It is an uphill battle, one I fight daily with myself, and that I hope to help my daughter win as she becomes a young woman. It will take lots of encouragement from me, her father, her teachers, and her mentors to teach her to beat down the voice of self-doubt, especially when everyone around her is telling her that she is just "average," and the awards are only given out to the superior few.

Christine asks me, "Are you happy with your life?," and it is easy for me to say, "Yes, I am very happy." I have a wonderful husband and children and I take great pleasure in my writing, my friends, good books, walking the dog, going to the art museum and to the movies. I am not particularly good at anything. But I laugh easily, I care about and love others deeply, and I know that my life is indeed blessed. I would have to say that my life is a success. I know that someday Christine will know the same about her own life.

So, when my daughter tells me she is not good at anything, sadly, by those impossible standards we set in high school, it's true. But, over time, the real measurement of success will win out. Christine will know that living and loving and caring are the real signs of a life well lived. And after her twenty-year high school reunion, I'll be waiting for her to call and say, "Mom, I really am good at a lot of things." Of course, she'll be right. And she won't need an award to prove it.

WHAT'S IN A NAME? PLENTY.

My name is Martha. Believe it or not, this was a difficult burden to bear while growing up in the 1960s. Surrounded by a sea of girls named Debbie, Nancy, or Linda, I was often asked: "Were you named after your aunt?" "Were you named after your grandma?" "Why did your parents name you that?" Even, "Do you like your name?" Well, no, I did not. On top of that, I was right smack dab in the middle of four sisters, all of whom were lucky enough to have what I perceived to be modern, lively-sounding names: Kathy, Julie, Susan, and Liz. My name, on the other hand, was different, not young and playful like a Tammy or a Jenny. Instead, it felt old-fashioned and stodgy.

As a child with an insecure shy streak, crooked teeth, and a gangly body towering over the Marys in my class, a name like Martha was certainly not an asset. I took on the burden of my name, and stayed quiet and in the background for the duration of my childhood.

I often asked my parents, "Why did you give me this name? Did you like it?" My parents' response was that of course they loved the name. Today, many people tell me they love my name. I still do not.

Naturally, as I was growing up, I made a vow that I would name my daughter the most classic, beautiful name that I could think of, a name that she would treasure. And when I gave birth to my daughter fifteen years ago, I did just that. I chose Christine. Turns out I chose wrong.

Almost from the time she could express an opinion, Christine has complained about her name. She laments that she is the only one with that name in her school, leaving me to wonder, just when did the name Christine go out of fashion? She complains that people call her Christina, which she loathes (I can relate; I am often called Marcia or Margaret, which I loathe). She wants to know why her dad and I named her that, and in a voice that echoes my parents', I say, "Because we loved the name." In fifth grade she switched schools and decided to go by Chris. The experiment failed: she hated the name Chris. Junior high brought the name Christy, and I kept my mouth shut even as I cringed. Visions of an air-headed cheerleader clouded my thoughts. I am certain there are many Christys out there with level heads and serious plans.

I have heard of people who treasure their unique names. I envy their sprit, and I wish I had more of it. Turns out my daughter feels the same way. History repeats itself, indeed.

This past year, on June 23rd, Christine turned fifteen and I turned fifty. On this day, as on many others, she proclaimed, "I have never felt like a Christine." Thinking that changing a name had to be a whole lot easier than changing a personality, or gender, or even a nose, I suggested she change it. I told her to pick a name she felt proud to own and proud to say and go to court and change it. But I had two conditions: first, we, her parents, had to like the name. Second, she would have to accept that we, her family, would always call her Christine. She agreed. In fact she said it would feel "weird" to have us call her by a different name.

And so, Christine went to court and officially became Allison. Christine is now her middle name. Allison Christine: it fits her just fine.

The reaction has been the most interesting part of this process. Some people applaud the action, cheering my bravery in making such a difficult decision. Others mistrust the decision: why let a fifteen-year-old girl make such a big life-changing choice? Others wonder how I must feel. After all, she is rejecting the very gift I gave her at birth. And still others wonder, does a person have the right to shed his or her name just as one would shed an old winter coat?

To all this I say, this act was neither brave nor foolish nor earth-shattering. If there is anything in this world that is bound up in a person's identity, it is surely one's name. We are our names; indeed, we are called by them dozens of times a day, and if the names don't fit or feel good, then we have the right to find something better.

And if the little baby I first held in my arms fifteen years ago says thanks but no thanks to the particular moniker I chose, that is just fine. It is *her* name after all.

When my husband, John, first learned of Allison's plans to legally change her name, he protested. How could she just reject the name she had carried all these years? I firmly told him that with his very classic, universally beloved name of John, he could never truly understand. I told him to trust me on this, and he did. As we stood in court that day, the judge asked John, "Why are you requesting this?" And he looked the judge straight in the eye and said, "It seems to us that it can only serve to boost her self-confidence if she goes by a name she likes." Turns out, he did understand.

I love the name Christine, and because I loved this newborn baby I gave her the gift of my favorite name. Now, fifteen years later, I'm happy to give her an even better gift: a new name, one that she wears with comfort. Allison Christine. She is Allison to the world, and Christine to us. And we are all happy.

A WORTHY WOMAN

Mother's Day is just around the corner, and I have to admit it: this holiday makes me ever so slightly uncomfortable. It makes me think of the mother in Hallmark commercials. She is smiling. She is calm. She is helpful. She has put the kids to bed without raising her voice. She is wearing makeup and her hair is combed. She is worthy of honor. I sometimes have to wonder if I am worthy.

When, after much pain and agony (they call it labor), I was handed this new baby and declared a mother, I expected a manual to arrive in the mail. In this manual it would tell me how to make a double batch of brownies for the school bake sale. There would be a section on making costumes for the church play. A chapter on doing the Girl Scout cookie order without screwing it up. It would have an entire section devoted to talking to your children rather than yelling at them. I would need to read this section twice.

Instead I was given nothing, short of free samples of Similac and Pampers.

I remember when my son was three years old; we learned he had an obstruction in his kidney, which would require major surgery. As we sat in the doctor's office discussing the prognosis, the different options, and various other medical decisions, I kept waiting for my own mother to walk in. I knew that *she* was the parent, in fact, had always been the parent, and that I was just sitting there because I had happened to give birth to this child. I hadn't yet officially been handed the instructions. What a surprise that they were actually asking *me* about this child's care.

But you know what? I did it. I was the mother. I asked good questions. I, along with my husband, made decisions regarding his care. I comforted our son through his tears, and I slept by his side in the hospital. And I didn't even need to look up how to do it.

Could it all be just trial and error? Does this really come without instructions? My friend Mary tells me you do your best, and if you mess up, just be sure to apologize at the end of the day. I have asked my children's forgiveness countless times.

My friend Rachel is pregnant with her first child. She told me that she would like to be a mother like me. I was shocked. Me? The one who has to call her own mother to ask her how to make lasagna for the potluck? The one that can barely sew a straight hem? The one that yells just a little too much? "Yes," she said, "because you look into your children's eyes and listen. You are compassionate and thoughtful. You are an advocate for your kids. You teach your children how to act around adults and other children. And most importantly, you laugh with them."

I guess I'm still a long way from the Hallmark model. But if they give out points for trying, I know I'll be at the top of the list in that department. And if they give out points for loving your kids, well, I'm king of the hill there too.

So, in honor of my great efforts, my undying love, and doing this all without a proper manual, I will let them honor me on Mother's Day. I will comb my hair; I will even put on makeup. I will try not to yell. And I will not squirm with discomfort. I am worthy.

SHE'S HAVING A BABY

Today's announcement: my sister is having a baby. My forty-nine-year-old, divorced, post-menopausal, corporate executive sister is having a baby. That is, she's *getting* a baby—all the way from China.

We are pleased. We are shocked. We are speechless. At least briefly.

I rush to call my friends, and their response is universal. "Forty-nine years old? Single? It makes me tired just to think about it. Does she have any idea what she is getting herself into?"

And I say, "No, she, in fact, probably has *no* idea."

But I know things about my big sister that they do not. I know that she entered college wearing a pleated skirt, and left college wearing overalls, a T-shirt, and no bra. I know that she walked through the riots and bombings while attending the University of Wisconsin in the early seventies. In fact, she is the only person I know that has been tear-gassed. I know that she has had friends die in the Vietnam War, and seen other friends die from cancer, diabetes, suicide, and even mountain climbing. She traveled to New York with a friend so that that friend could get an abortion, at a time when that was the only state where it was legal. She has put up with a philandering husband, a messy divorce, abusive boyfriends, and restraining orders to keep a stalker at bay. On top of all that, she has fought to stay sober for eleven years now, fought the glass ceiling at every corporate job she's entered, and fought a court battle when she was unjustly fired. Like all women her age, she has fought the good fight all the way. She's been battered and bruised, but come out swinging. From the time she drove from Wisconsin to California in her Chevy Vega, she has seen and done things I've only heard about. I live my rebel life through her.

She tells me it's ironic. She always thought that she would be the one to stay home, happily married, with lots of kids. Somehow life, or maybe it was just the times she grew up in, threw that vision off course. So, she's given up on the husband, the domestic life, but she hasn't given up on the kid. She's not going to give up on a dream that she has kept in her heart since childhood.

They say that these girls from China have been rejected by their parents because they are daughters, not sons. They are left on the roadside, in trash containers, in produce bins at the market. These rejected girls are then taken in and brought to the United States, into the arms of a family who wants and loves them completely and without reservation.

And so it will be with my sister. She will take this rejected girl; let her know that life is tough, but that she will get through it. Heaven knows she has the experience from which to draw her motherly advice.

As I was leaving the dinner table, someone said something about a baby shower. The picture was just too incongruous. My sister: tough, wise, and often a little bitchy, surrounded by fuzzy pink bears and a new diaper bag.

But what the heck? Why not throw her a party? She's made it through all the other things life has thrown at her. Chances are she'll find a way to make it through late night feedings, potty training, and school conferences too. I sure hope so. Because I must admit, it does make me tired just to think about it.

BY THE BEAUTIFUL SEA

"By the sea, by the sea, by the beautiful sea…"

Well, the long, tedious task of unpacking the bags is almost complete. The sandy shoes have been rinsed off, the life jackets and snorkels stowed away until next year, and the piles of laundry have been cleaned and folded. We have returned from no less daunting than that most dreaded of all events: the family reunion. Yes, we survived and are all still in one piece. I'm still unpacking my own bags—the ones in my head filled with amazement and wonder about this past week's experience.

"You and me, you and me, oh how happy we'll be…"

My parents celebrated their fiftieth wedding anniversary this summer. They had warned us a few years ago that they wished to celebrate by having all of us vacation together at a resort by the ocean for four whole days. If you knew the family from which I sprung, you would understand why this was a warning. Let's just start with the demographics. Five girls. No boys. You get the picture. More hormones and tears and catfights arose from this little tribe on Greenfield Street than from a sheik's harem. And in the ensuing years, this little bunch suffered further from jealousy, estrangement, depression, alcoholism, divorce, job layoffs, and just a big dose of animosity between various warring factions. That my parents would have the courage, some might say the audacity, to bring this clan together to "have some fun" seemed ludicrous.

But we did it. As a gift to the parents who wanted us to be together, we all said yes. No expectations, other than to get through the week intact. If the kids had fun playing in the ocean and on the beach, well, that would be a little side benefit. The goal here was simply survival.

"When each wave comes a rollin' in, we will duck or swim..."

All I can say is, thank God for kids. Because all they want is to have fun. They love their cousins. They love to play kickball and to swim. And they don't care who likes whom, and who did what to whom all those years ago. They know that anger and resentment mean nothing when you're trying to build a sand castle.

So, we lumbering adults followed their lead, playing along right next to them. And we did OK. We really did. Oh, there were the requisite petty arguments, the gossip spoken in loud whispers on pillows at night, the rekindled resentments. But there too was some laughter (actually, quite a bit of laughter), some conversation, some fun, and I daresay some connection we hadn't allowed ourselves to feel in years.

"And we'll float and fool around the water. Over and under, and then up for air..."

Each night this large group of adults and children trudged into the resort dining room and seated ourselves at the long table set to accommodate us all. On the last night we were together, my parents stood up at the end of the meal, and arm in arm sang "By the Beautiful Sea." As they were singing, I looked over at my sisters and their families. The husbands seemed a bit dazed by the performance, the kids either mesmerized or oblivious. But the sisters were another story. Not a dry eye in the house. Even an old cynic like me had to wipe away a few tears. It seems this big old tattered boat might just stay pieced together with shreds of happiness, connectedness, and even a little bit of pain and resentment.

"Pa is rich, ma is rich, so now what do we care..."

I will finish the unpacking today, but my thoughts will linger for a long time to come. It is with wonder and gratitude and even sadness that I look at this group of sisters. Yes, I think this big old ship will survive. More holes are bound to appear over the years, but maybe a few more patches will appear too. Like it or not, we are all a part of it, our link ordained by our birth, our connection determined by our willingness to at least try to be a family, whatever that might mean. There is already talk of next year's reunion. We'll wait and see what the new year brings for us all. Maybe it was enough that we survived this year. And survive, we did.

"I love to be beside your side, beside the sea, beside the seaside, by the beautiful sea!"

ABOUT THE AUTHOR

Martha Wegner lives and writes in St. Paul, Minnesota. She is the author of numerous articles and books, including the memoir, *Dear David: Dealing with My Son's Addiction One Letter at a Time* (Beaver's Pond Press). For more information, visit her website at www.marthawegner.com.